UNLOCK YOUR GOD-CONFIDENCE WORKBOOK FOR WOMEN

Copyright © 2023 by Ellen Reimer
Kelowna BC Canada

All rights reserved. No part of this publication may be reproduced, distributed, or transmitted in any form or by any means, including photocopying, recording, or other electronic or mechanical methods, without the prior written permission of the publisher, except in the case of brief quotations embodied in critical reviews and certain other noncommercial uses permitted by copyright law. For permission requests, write to the publisher, addressed "Attention: Permissions Coordinator," at the link below.

https://www.inspiredcounselling.ca/contact

Ordering Information:
Quantity sales. Special discounts are available on quantity purchases by corporations, associations, and others. For details, contact the publisher at the link above.

Every effort has been made to cite, acknowledge, trace or contact all copyright holders. The publisher/author will be pleased to make good any omissions or rectify any mistakes brought to their attention at the earliest opportunity.

The author is providing this book and its contents on an "as is" basis and make no representations or warranties of any kind with respect to this book or its contents. The publisher author disclaims all such representations and warranties, including but not limited to warranties of healthcare for a particular purpose. In addition, t he author assume no responsibility for errors, inaccuracies, omissions, or any other inconsistencies herein.

The content of this book is for informational purposes only and is not intended to diagnose, treat, cure, or prevent any condition, illness or disease. You understand that this book is not intended as a substitute for consultation with a licensed practitioner. Please consult with your own physician or healthcare specialist regarding the suggestions and recommendations made in this book. The use of this book implies your acceptance of this disclaimer.

The author makes no guarantees concerning the level of success you may experience by following the advice and strategies contained in this book, and you accept the risk that results will differ for each individual. The testimonials and examples provided in this book show exceptional results, which may not apply to the average reader, and are not intended to represent or guarantee that you will achieve the same or similar results.

For general information on our other products, resources and services or to obtain technical support, please contact us at the link below;
https://www.inspiredcounselling.ca/contact

Printed Canada

Unlock Your God Confidence Workbook
ISBN 978-1-7388453-0-9

Self Published

First Paperback Edition 2023

https://www.inspiredcounselling.ca/

Editor: Brittany Gale
Portrait Photo by Jenna Gibbs Photography
Illistrations used under licence from Canva

UNLOCK YOUR GOD-CONFIDENCE WORKBOOK FOR WOMEN

**A WORKBOOK FOR WOMEN, DESIGNED TO:
EMBRACE YOUR MESSY
UNLOCK YOUR GREATEST POTENTIAL
KNOW GOD'S EXTRAVAGANT LOVE
BE BOLD & LIVE FULLY ALIVE**

Ellen Reimer RPC. CLC

Acknowledgements

My life as it is would not be possible without the amazing humans that have been a part of my life, whom I'd like to acknowledge and thank.

First, I'd like to thank my four sons for your unwavering belief in me and encouraging me to continue. You have taught me so much since the day you each were born. "I love you each so much".

I thank my dearest friends for continued encouragement, support, care, constructive criticism and love as I applied each of the tools in this book to my own life as I took my own healing journey.

I thank my extended family and friends for your heartfelt support, advice, perspectives, friendship, and walking the meandering path of life with me.

I thank the counselors and coaches in my life (you know who you are) for your support, encouragement, listening ear, inspiration, sincerity, patience, prayers and dedication to my healing journey. For the tools you have provided to me for getting me to where I am today.

Finally, I'd like to thank you, my cherished readers. To have the words of this workbook brought to life in your own healing journey is humbling, an honor, rewarding and a gift beyond measure.

Thank you from the bottom of my heart. I am genuinely and forever grateful!

About

This book is designed to promote healing, by inviting Jesus into the painful places of your heart, find forgiveness and walk fully in God's goodness, love and His design for us.

This course will walk you through steps of **God-discovery, self-discovery and acceptance** for who you are and for your story.

Each chapter is built on the next, created to encourage reflection, healing, courage and hope. You will begin a journey of self reflection, processing negative core beliefs and where they originated from, forgiveness and inviting Jesus into the pain, and exploring the gifts, strengths and beauty God created you with.

The tools used in this workbook have been used by Ellen personally in her own journey to healing. Her hope is that you also will find healing, joy, hope and God's extravagant love for you.

WELCOME

Content

1. Introduction — 11
2. Younger You — 25
3. Belief Debunker - Redesign Your Thoughts — 35
4. Architect Of Your Story — 53
5. Power In Forgiveness — 63
6. Designing Your Road-Map — 79
7. Life Compass — 93
8. You Shine — 108
9. Mining Deeper For Gold — 125
10. Beautiful Authentic You — 141

A message from the author

"Do you ever feel like life is just painful or hard? Maybe messy is a better word to describe it?

I know I have felt that way in my life, my description of it would be painful, hard, messy, really messy sometimes, or a lot of the time and stuck...very stuck.

So I personally went on a journey to get unstuck...and even that was messy as I processed pain and heart ache and lots of tears.

As you go on this step by step journey of exploring your blocks, limiting beliefs, my hope is that you will find healing and discover the amazing and beautiful human God created you to be.

Unlock your God-Confidence is designed to help you embrace your messy, unlock your greatest potential and know God's extravagant love for you! You will spend the next few weeks unpacking what holds you back, the negative narratives you tell yourself and will be guided through a process of self-discovery and self-acceptance for you and for your story, gaining hope and tools for overcoming negative self-talk.

You will kick low-self esteem in the butt, grab a hold of boldness and confidence as you come to know the great potential that lies within you.

You are embarking on a journey that will bring healing and wholeness, unlock the greatness within you and allow yourself to begin joyfully living the wild and precious life you have been given.

You will discover the confidence to let your true self shine and gain the keys that create personal breakthrough, healing, wholeness and live FULLY ALIVE!

Unlock Your God-Confidence is designed with a perspective of God's extravagant love for you and the beautiful woman He created you to be.

This workbook is designed to be processed over 10 weeks – I encourage you to take the time to reflect and process each exercise as they are placed here for a purpose and reason. Each week you will take another step toward healing and gaining a deeper understanding of yourself and who God made you to be.

You may also enjoy taking this jounce with a friend or in a group for added support and accountability.

I know that my personal journey was not always easy...yes there were lots of messy and hard days, but I am so grateful I took the steps towards healing and that is my hope for you. To learn who you really are, that beautiful and amazing heart and soul that you have and let the boldness that you may have hidden away have a chance to be seen. To turn your messy into a message of hope and joy."

I pray the next few weeks of reflection and looking inward are insightful, healing and a time to gain a greater understanding of God's great love for you.

Love,

Ellen

> "Now I know that I am for my Beloved
> and all His desires are fulfilled in me."
> song of songs 7:10

VERSE OF THE DAY

CHAPTER ONE
INTRODUCTION

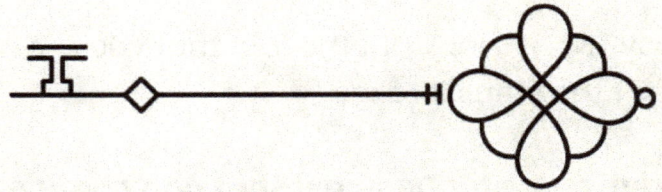

WHO AM I?

Have you ever asked yourself Who AM I? Have you wondered why you are here on this earth and longed for a deeper knowing of yourself? Have you sensed there is more to life and it is just out of reach?

This course will walk you through steps of **God-discovery, self-discovery and acceptance** for who you are and for your story. Our stories do not need to define us, but they do help to shape us. **Discover your strengths and the beauty that lies within you. Discover the beautiful woman that you are designed and created to be by our Heavenly Father - Papa.**

Life has painful moments from childhood, teen years or adulthood, that can leave you feeling crushed, overwhelmed with memories and emotions, a lack of direction and purpose and feelings of being stuck forever in a limiting pattern, and often leave a person feeling alone and unknown, wondering if God is real.

I too have been there. I clearly recall the day I stood in my kitchen with tears streaming down my cheeks and cried out 'who am I?".

Many of the steps in this program have been powerful tools in overcoming my own insecurities and lack of identity and not having a clue how much my Heavenly Father loves me. I understand the deep need to know who we are at the core of our being. I promise you also can experience the joy and empowerment in being ok with you, in knowing your worth and value and that **your uniqueness is beautiful and needed in this world.** You too can **discover how Jesus loves you so much** and that in knowing Him, trusting Him and **having a deeper relationship with Him is where your truest self-shines.**

"See what great love the Father has lavished on us, that we should be called children of God! And that is what we are!" - 1 John 3:1 NIV

Is it easy? No, it is not, but the fact that you are here tells me that you have a desire and are ready for the steps it takes.

You have a Master Designer that can change your lives. but it is you who gets to invite Him into that place in your life. With His lavish and divine love, with His help, the only person who can change your life is you, and it's going to require effort.

But the effort is worth it.

The questions below are strategic, personal and powerful to begin the process of discovering more about yourself. We often live on autopilot, without tuning in to questions and details about ourselves. Enjoy this exercise, there are a lot of questions. Don't stress over the questions but rather approach them with a curiosity for yourself and for how God sees you.

GETTING TO KNOW YOU

1. What 5 words describe you the best?

2. What words best describe how you believe Jesus sees you?

3. What makes you happy?

4. What makes you sad or angry?

5. What is your energy drainer and makes you tired?

6. What scares you the most in life?

7. What are your hobbies? What hobbies have you have dreamt of doing but have not started yet?

8. 5 words your friends or family use to describe you?

9. What are your negative habits?

10. What are you most proud of in life?

11. What are your top 3 achievements in life?

12. What are your top 3 disappointments in life?

13. Who inspires you?

14. Using 5 words, who do you want to be in life?

15. What is the most important thing in my life?

16. Who are the most important people in my life?

17. What's my definition of success?

18. How do I want others to see me?

19. What is one dream you have that you have never shared with anyone?

20. What do you believe is God's purpose for you?

God has names for each of us. He has names He calls you – What do you hear Him whisper when He gently says your name?

REFLECTION

What insight did you gain about yourself that surprised you while answering the above questions?

Did you discover anything new about yourself?

How does it feel to discover and reflect on yourself?

God made you uniquely you, with your unique personality, likes and dislikes, your smile and your beautiful heart. He invites you to get to know this amazing wonder that He created.

HOW SELF-AWARE ARE YOU?

Part of this journey is developing self-awareness. Self-awareness allows for you to be more in-tune with your beliefs, thoughts and actions.

You have the ability and willpower within you to choose and to raise your awareness levels. Raising your awareness levels will bring more clarity, authenticity, vulnerability, beauty and courage to your personal, spiritual, business/career life as well as in your relationships. Raising your awareness will require persistence and patience with yourself. It is a lifelong journey of continuing to work the self-aware muscle and having a willingness to grow and a curiosity for life.

Self-awareness is key to personal growth and discovering deeper meaning and more about yourself and about your relationship with Jesus.

Greek philosopher Aristotle expressed it this way –

"Knowing yourself is the beginning of all wisdom."

Self-awareness is important but is also one of the most difficult skills to master and there is no one secret answer that is going to work for everyone as 'a one size fits all'. Everybody is different and you are going to be your best teacher in developing self-awareness.

It's called self-awareness for a reason. It's about you.
It's about getting to know yourself on a deeper level.
It's about **getting really curious about who you are as a person and who God says you are.**
It's about finding an awareness and quiet place that allows you to hear God whisper His lavish love for you over your life.

What does self-awareness mean to you?

Chapter 1 | Introduction

You're uncovering which things about yourself are going to help you grow as a person and which things are harmful and damaging to you as a person.

One of the ways to become more self-aware is mindfulness.

I have struggled with the word mindfulness and with practicing it, however, I find it to be a very beneficial and important part of my everyday life for self-awareness and personal growth and most importantly for hearing God.

Let's take a moment to focus on mindfulness and do a body scan relaxation check. Research suggests that meditation promotes self-awareness, encouraging self-acceptance and compassion towards yourself.

- Find a space that is quiet and comfortable. Put on some relaxing music if you choose.
- Begin by bringing your attention into your body.
- You can close your eyes if that's comfortable for you.
- Notice your body seated or lying down, feeling the weight of your body on the chair, the bed or the floor.
- Take a few deep breaths.
- And as you take a deep breath, bring in more oxygen and picture yourself in your favorite place, (nature, a quiet room). And as you exhale, let your body relax more deeply.
- Notice your feet, notice the sensations of your feet touching the floor. The weight and pressure, hot or cold sensations, the vibrations
- Notice your legs - pressure, pulsing, heaviness, lightness.
- Notice your back against the floor, chair or bed.
- How does your stomach feel? Is it tense or tight, let it soften? Take a breath. Notice the rise and fall of your stomach as you continue to breath in and out.
- Notice your hands. Are your hands tense or tight? Can you let your hands loosen their grip and soften?
- Feel any sensation in your arms.
- Let your shoulders be soft.
- Notice your neck and throat. Let them be soft. Relax.
- Soften your jaw. Let your face and facial muscles soften.
- Then notice your whole-body present. Take another deep breath.
- Be aware of your whole body. Take a deep breath. When you are ready, you can open your eyes.

What do you notice? Do you feel any difference? Do you feel more present and aware?

This takes patience and practice. The benefits of daily relaxation and/or mediation are great and definitely worth the time. **Take time to tune into you, and into your surroundings.** I have many times done a quick check-in while in nature walking or hiking.

- Pause
- Take three deep breaths
- Focus on your 4 senses, one at a time
    - What do I feel?
    - What do you see?
    - What do I smell?
    - What do I hear?

This short exercise calms the mind and brings me back into awareness and grounds me.

During the time we are together for this course I would like to encourage you to practice mindfulness every day. Rate yourself today at the beginning of the course of how mindful and aware you feel, how present you feel and at the completion of our time together, practicing every day, rate yourself again and notice any changes that may have occurred.

Not Present All   Somewhat Present   Full Present & Aware

1_____5_____10

LIFE INVENTORY

In the following exercise, picture each line / scale as a ladder in your life. This is not a time for you to judge yourself but rather to just become aware of all the specific areas of your life. **Awareness opens the door to change and to growth.** What we do not know, we cannot change, where there is not change, there is not growth. Awareness and change is an opportunity for growth and **a life of thriving and joy.** In the line / scale, mark where you feel you are today, not where you want to be. But where you are currently.

Relationships - how satisfied are you with the relationships in your life? (Friendships, romantic, family)

1_____10

Environment - Your physical surroundings (where you live, neighbors, relatives, colleagues)

1_____10

Career - How satisfied are you with your job, profession, business, (the way you earn an income)

1_____10

Money - Income, Expenses, Savings and Investments

1_____10

Personal Growth - how satisfied are you with the time you spend on self-development? (time you spend on continued education, reading, open mindedness, coaching, counselling)

1_____10

Enjoyment/brightness of life - what is the level of enjoyment you get from life? (pleasure, relaxation, hobbies, travel, entertainment)

1_____10

Spirituality / Faith - How satisfied or content are you with your spiritual life? (your relationship with Jesus, the time you take be with Him, how known you feel by Him) Healthy - how is your satisfaction with your health? (mental/emotional, physical, exercise, energy, nutrition)

1_____10

Reflect for a moment as you observe where you are on each ladder. Are you thriving or surviving? Are there areas of your life that you would like to change to begin thriving in this area?

Everything is interconnected. When one category suffers the others suffer. Finding a balance in each area of your life will bring you a real sense of fulfillment and wellbeing.

My hope is that throughout this course, your life will become balanced and full. Approaching life with curiosity and attention will be a game changer for you. During the rest of the course, have a curiosity for you...

a curiosity for the amazing and beautiful human being that you are.

I look forward to spending the next few weeks with you as you delve into exploring and discovering more about your true self. Invite Jesus into this moment and into your journey in discovering more about yourself and how He sees you. Invite compassion and curiosity as your constant companions into unlocking the greatness that lies within you.

SELF-CARE
What does self-care mean to you?

Part of self-care is self-compassion and curiosity. This week get curious, about what you love to do, what brings you joy, what makes you laugh... and then go do it.

HOMEWORK
Find an accountability partner for this journey that you have begun.

It is easy to give up the journey, feel afraid of the discomfort of unfamiliar emotions or to just need a friend / mentor to process out loud to. Find someone that you trust and feel safe with, invite them on this journey with you and to hold you accountable to continue when the going gets tough. Find someone that will listen when you need a listening ear and will encourage and support you.

MY PRAYER FOR YOU TODAY
"Papa, I lift this beautiful woman to you, her name you know. Papa, I ask that you bless her throughout her life and especially in the next weeks as she begins to uncover Your great love for her. Open her eyes and her ears, let her fully know what intimate relationship with you feels like. Let her know the worth and value you place on her so she may rise up and claim the heavenly inheritance you have her. Today, Papa, let her feel your arms embrace her and lavish her with a love she has never experienced before and that she continues to hunger for.

Thank you, Papa, for the beauty in her.

Amen"

"And so, we know and rely on the love God has for us. God is love. Whoever lives in love lives in God, and God in them." 1 John 4:16 NIV

CHAPTER TWO
YOUNGER YOU

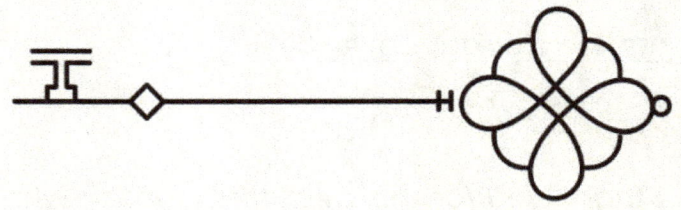

GROUNDING EXERCISE

Find a space to relax and get comfortable - put some soaking music on if you prefer.

- Pause
- Close your eyes
- Picture a peaceful place, either in real life or an imaginary place in your mind.
- Invite Jesus into the picture... Where is He? *(holding you, dancing with you, carrying you or walking to meet you?)*
- Take five deep breaths *(with each inhale, breath in the peace, with each exhale, picture the stresses of the day leaving your body)*
- Focus on your 4 senses, one at a time
    - What do I feel?
    - What do you see?
    - What do I smell?
    - What do I hear?

Notice how you feel after you have completed this grounding exercise. Notice the muscle tension, has it been released? This breathing exercise is meant to ground you in preparation for today's module.

SONG OF THE DAY

Before we delve into the next segment - prepare your heart for more by listening to music. Below is a song suggestion *by Chris Tomlin* that has been chosen for you. Be still and let the music and words speak to you.

Chris Tomlin - Nobody Loves Me Like You

PRAYER

"Papa, I thank you for this beautiful woman who has found her way here today. Bless her as she processes. Let her feel your tender love for her, pour your love over her and hold her close to your heart, let her hear your heartbeat for her today. Amen."

LET'S BEGIN

You have spent some time in the introduction asking yourself some questions and gaining some knowledge about you that you may tend to take for granted, things you do and think without really 'thinking' about them.

But now comes the hard work, digging deeper.

Can you **give yourself permission to put away any mask** that you may have on, any pretense, and come out of hiding for this course, especially today as you look at your younger self. That younger you.

When you stay in hiding and do not acknowledge that young child, so innocent and sweet, but yet hurting; negative beliefs and behaviors continue to have power and control, holding you back from discovering **the greatness God has put in you**.

Read the following verse from Genesis 12:2 written for you –

> *"And I will make of you a great nation, and I will bless you and make your name great, so that you will be a blessing."*

It can be difficult to believe these words apply to ourselves, but '**He desires to make your name great, to bless you'.** Way too often we push aside the goodness that He wants to give us because we feel we are not worthy or that the 'blessings' are for someone else.

When a core belief is formed as a child it becomes a filter through which all life experiences are processed through. It is like wearing a pair of glasses with a blue lens, all of life appears blue, if you wear brown lenses then the world will appear brown. Hence if you were neglected as a child and a belief was formed that you are unlovable because you were not given the loving attention you as a child needed and deserved you will go through life looking at every experience with the belief that you are 'unlovable'. You will believe that you have to be a certain way to be valued and loved, this belief will flow into how you perceive our Heavenly Papa sees you and how much He loves you.

Thus, if you want to change your life as an adult, **it is vital to change the belief system,** the lens through which you look, finding a new core belief - your truth and the truth of how God sees you. To do this, it is important to connect with your younger self. That little girl or boy that you were. To give yourself permission to grieve and experience healing.

Grieving is an important part of the journey to finding our true sense of self as we grieve the pain the younger you experienced. We cannot finish the past without the ability to grieve.

***Every child needs to know that they are loved unconditionally.** Loved without judgment and to know that they matter and are significant, that they can trust their caretakers and are safe.*

The Inner Child needs **gentleness and compassion** as you go on this journey through childhood memories of the heart and to connect with the child within.

Picture yourself in a safe place and invite Jesus to walk with you through the memories, How does He see that little girl?

Let yourself love and be curious... have you met your inner child? Can you have compassion and curiosity for her/him?

Your inner child is the **truest and most authentic core of your being**. The youngest and most innocent part of you that has been hidden away. As you picture your younger self, imagine, how would Jesus look at that little girl?

This younger version of you is also the part of you that took on beliefs about yourself that cause fear, insecurity and shame. **Every experience is shaped by these beliefs.**

When your inner child is neglected, she withers away, burying creativity, vitality, expressiveness and energy within. When the needs of the child are left unresolved, it is a pain, which as an adult, is then acted out, some people refer to this as the 'shadow self' or 'wounded inner child'.

When the pain of the wounded child is left unattended, you tend to bury the energy and expressiveness of the inner child, missing out on the playfulness, trust relationships, joy, belly laughs, spontaneity, bliss, awe, wonder and the soul/heart connections and instead act out of the wounded inner child or shadow self, feeling depressed, anxious, angry, frustrated, isolated, reserved, shy, alone. You may struggle with codependency, toxic relationships, unhealthy boundaries and a lack of communication skills. There is often a belief formed that God is not available to you, He doesn't love you and He doesn't care. Sometimes this belief takes on the form of a God that is condemning and a mean judgmental God.

The effects of the wounded inner child reach far and wide into every aspect of life and will be found in many forms of pain impacting you physically, mentally, emotionally and spiritually.

The younger you simply wanted and longed **to be loved and held in a safe space** by the caretakers and most significant people in your life. And that young you is still longing to be held by love and acceptance. To be given permission to just be you...

To know that you are deeply loved by Father God and to experience the world with openness and wonder, while having the confidence in your adult self to have the wisdom that life experiences bring.

This Journey is not easy and may be very painful for you. Have compassion for yourself and if you are not ready for this step, that is ok. Skip to the next session or contact your counselor to help you work through this process. If you do not have one, we offer on-line counselling and coaching and can be contacted at www.inspiredcounselling.ca/contact

We are all on a journey and at different places of healing and it is ok to feel uncomfortable for this step.

My first step into healing my inner child and learning love and acceptance for myself as a woman was finding a picture of myself when I was 1.5 years old. Oh the sweetness and innocence with childlike, wide-eyed wonder.

Your first step to healing in this module is to find a picture of your younger self. That little girl or boy...the one that makes you smile with love today. The one that, if you met that little girl in the park, you would want to give her a hug and tell her how adorable she is with her dimples and messy, windblown hair.

(I would encourage finding 2 or 3 pictures at different stages of your life. A toddler, school age and teenager.)

> *"But Jesus said, "Let the little children come to me and do not hinder them, for to such belongs the kingdom of heaven." Mathew 19:14*

JOURNALING

Take some time for this exercise. Create space and time to be alone, find a place that feels safe where you can let yourself feel the emotions, put on your favorite music and let yourself relax into this time with compassion and curiosity.

Look into the eyes of that little child. What do you see? What would you say to that little girl, little boy today if you saw them on the playground or building a sandcastle on the beach? Look at the teen with curiosity and compassion, what would you say to that young teenager trying so hard to fit in?

What does that little girl need to hear from you today? How beautiful she is… how you love her spunkiness…What else?

What does the teenager, so desperately needing acceptance and validation need to hear from you?

What did she not get back then, that today you can give her? What is she longing to hear? What would make her laugh in delight?

Think about what you loved to do as a child. Take a walk down memory lane… did you like to climb trees? maybe you built tree forts? Rock collections or building towns in the sandbox? Did you enjoy riding bikes with friends, or reading a favorite story book? Did you have a favorite cuddling stuffy or a pet? What was your favorite food? Who was your favorite person? That safe place?

Allow yourself to go on a journey with your younger self by asking some questions and allowing yourself to feel the emotions and thoughts that you experience in this process. It is ok to feel messy at this time. That is why you chose a safe and quiet spot to journal this process. be patient, be loving, kind and accepting.

When was the first time you felt scared?

When did you first feel unsafe? Unloved? Lonely?

It may be easier to do an imagery walk down memory lane.

Relax, close your eyes and breathe deeply.

Imagine you're walking down a pathway through a field of grass and wildflowers. This field is a safe place where you feel loved and secure. Soak in your surroundings, what does it feel like? Smell like and look like?

Imagine a small child coming down the pathway or running through the grass towards you. This child is your younger self. You open your arms and give the small child a gentle bear hug and gently set them down beside you on a picnic blanket, maybe this young child, younger you is sitting safely tucked in your arms

When you're ready, ask the small child the questions you would like to ask?

- "When was the first time you/I felt sad or scared?"

- When did you first feel lonely? Rejected? Abandoned? neglected?

- Deep inside you, you may hear an answer, a knowing.

- Have compassion for the small child, hold him/her gently

- What would you as the adult like to say to the young child now?

- Make sure you hug them, thank them, and tell them how much they mean to you.

- Say goodbye to them.

- Leave the field of grass and wildflowers

- Open your eyes and tune into how you are feeling, the emotions and thoughts you are experiencing.

Some places may be too painful to imagine walking into.

You may have experienced abuse, pain no child, girl or woman should ever experience. Neglect. I am sorry this has happened to you. I am sorry you did not receive the love you deserved. The safety.

Give yourself some space to acknowledge the pain, the sorrow, the anger. Can you let yourself grieve the loss or lack? It was wrong! Picture your little girl self and be compassionate with her, give her some empathy.

As adults, we view the world very differently than we did as little children. Oftentimes, what we view as insignificant as an adult was painful and left deep scars in the child. It may be a parent that was always at work, being bullied in school, an emotionally distant parent, a controlling or manipulative caregiver, adult responsibilities and worries at too young of an age, words that were not supportive, words that should have been said but were not, eg. you are beautiful, I love you, abuse - emotionally, physically, sexually, spiritually. These all, as significant or insignificant as they may seem, have an effect on our childhood and we carry this into adulthood.

These exercises are not to berate caregivers, but to bring awareness to your emotional childhood map. Through gently exploring your childhood and connecting with your younger self, you open yourself up for opportunity to grieve, beginning the healing process from pain that you have unconsciously or consciously been holding on to for years. Unmet needs and repressed childhood emotions, along with a childlike enthusiasm and innocence, creativity, playfulness, sensitivity and wonder lie within you waiting to be set free.

This journey into healing will allow you to open yourself up to claiming that part of you that has been hidden for so many years, to fully walk into your passions and live uninhibited. By connecting with your younger self, or inner child you connect with feelings that have been suppressed and causing challenges as an adult, bringing these feelings to awareness allows you to focus on the root cause of your challenges, insecurities, limiting beliefs and lack of self-confidence and identity.

Transformation takes place deep within us as expression and voice is given to the 'inner child' and suppressed emotions.

Journal your thoughts and feelings. There is no right or wrong to this exercise, just give yourself permission to look at that delightful younger version of you with curiosity and love. If you are struggling to connect to this exercise... think of a child you know today, maybe your child, a niece or nephew, godchild or a friends child. What would you say to them if their story was like yours? What do they need?

DIGGING DEEPER

You have taken a walk down memory lane and likely feel emotional and tired by now, wondering if this is really worth all the feels you are feeling. This has been hard and painful to remember, and yet so important. Be proud of yourself for taking this step.

We have another exercise in this session that may be hard to do. **Take a short break,** make yourself a cup of tea, or go for a short walk, then **create some time and space.**

When you are ready, and only when you are ready I am asking you to write a letter to your parents, caregiver, guardian. The adult in your life that you experienced pain from. You may need to write more than one letter. It may be to 2 or 3 individuals, but write, **UNCENSORED**. This is not a time for politeness, this is a time **to say everything** that you did not get to say as a child but needed to. Everything you have wanted to say but couldn't, as you were growing up.

Let yourself be angry, mad, cry. Let yourself grieve what you didn't have, what you lost, the neglect or abuse, This is **not a time to censor your writing,** there may come a day when you want to write the letter censored but for today this one's for you to write all those suppressed emotions, feelings, thoughts on paper, to give your younger self and now adult self a chance to say what you have not been able to express. To give yourself a voice. This letter will not be sent to anyone at this time, but rather it is the beginning of your journey to healing.

What came up for you during this letter writing?

Were there emotions and feelings that surprised you?

You may feel that now is a time to talk with your counsellor about the experiences and trauma you may have gone through.

Take time to ground yourself.

Take 3 - 4 deep breaths, picturing a peaceful, safe place as you breathe in and the tension and negative emotions flowing out as you let go of the breath.

Take notice:
- What do you smell?
- What do you see?
- What do you hear?
- What do you feel?

SELF-CARE

Be gentle and compassionate to yourself. Self-care is vital in the healing and discovery journey you have embarked on. Take a walk in nature or a hot bath with candles, do for you what gives you a sense of well-being.Be proud of yourself for starting on this journey to healing and taking the difficult steps that you did today.

What will you do for selfcare today? This week?

HOMEWORK

Keep a picture of that adorable younger you on the fridge or dresser, somewhere that you can see her every day. Throughout the duration of this course, what can you incorporate into your activities that you loved to do as a child? Or that you dreamed of doing?

You stepped outside of the comfort zone today and that is where growth takes place and change happens. I am so proud of you for being willing to go deep today!

MY PRAYER FOR YOU TODAY

"Heavenly Papa, You know the pain this beautiful woman has walked through as a child, a teen, a young woman and as an adult. Pain that felt like it was crushing her, pain that made her feel like she was always in the wrong, that she is deserving of hurt and ridicule, possibly name calling and bullying, left her feeling invisible, unseen, unknown, not enough, and unlovable. Wrap your loving strong arms around her today, I pray that she feels Your gentle invitation to rest her head on your chest and to rest there. I pray that she can envision her younger self and how sweet and adorable that little girl is. Innocent yet full of life, spunkiness, and fun. Jesus, open her heart to receive your love... and where there is a crust that has been there to protect her, pour out your healing oil to heal those wounds where she has been so deeply hurt. And Papa, if she has not experienced Your love in a tangible way before, if she does not know You, reveal yourself to her in this moment and throughout her journey in this course. Amen"

INVITATION

I want to take this time to Invite you, if you have never given your heart to Jesus, to do so now if you wish to make Jesus your Lord and Savior. This is not a necessary step for the course, but I can promise you it will change your life if you choose to. It is a life-giving choice. He is always waiting with outstretched hands for You, inviting each of us in. If you want to invite Him into your heart pray this prayer with me now.

"Dear Lord Jesus, I need you, Thank you for dying on the cross for my sins, I believe You died for my sins and rose from the dead. I open the door of my life and receive You as my Savior and Lord. I turn from my sins and invite You to come into my heart and life. Make me the kind of person you want me to be. I want to trust and follow You as my Lord and Savior. In Your Name. Amen"

If you prayed the above prayer and invited Jesus into your heart and life, Welcome into Gods family, you are His child, an heir of the Royal family.

> *"But you are a chosen race, a royal priesthood, a holy nation, a people for his own possession, that you may proclaim the excellencies of him who called you out of darkness into his marvelous light." 1 Peter 2:9*

Find a mentor, a bible study or a bible-based church that you can learn and grow
Spend time daily talking with God, He really does love spending time with you.

If you prayed this prayer for the first time, or if you are just feeling alone in your God journey, email Ellen at inspiredcounselling@gmail.com. I would love to hear your story and would be more than happy to help you connect to a community of like-minded women for you to learn and grow with.

CHAPTER THREE
REDESIGN YOUR THOUGHTS

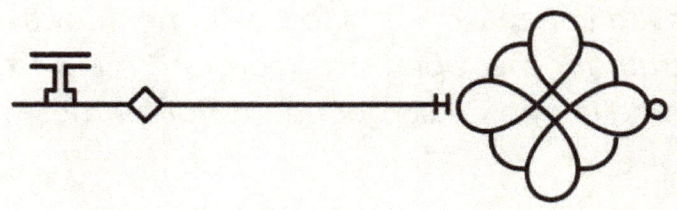

GROUNDING EXERCISE

Find a space to relax and get comfortable - put some soaking music on **to still your soul and mind.**

- Pause
- Close your eyes
- Picture a peaceful place, either in real life or an imaginary place in your mind.
- Invite Jesus into the picture… Where is He? *(holding you, dancing with you, carrying you or walking to meet you?)*
- Take five deep breaths *(with each inhale, breath in the peace, with each exhale, picture the stresses of the day leaving your body)*
- Focus on your 4 senses, one at a time
    - What do I feel?
    - What do you see?
    - What do I smell?
    - What do I hear?

Notice how you feel after you have completed this grounding exercise. Notice the muscle tension, has it been released? This breathing exercise is meant to ground you in preparation for today's module.

SONG OF THE DAY

Prepare your heart for more by listening to **the suggested worship** music. Below is a song **by Lauren Daigle** that has been chosen for you. Be still and let the music and words speak to you.

[Lauren Daigle – You Say](#)

PRAYER

"Jesus, I invite you to walk and talk with me, sit with me as I go through this module. Show me your truth for me. Open my heart and mind to your voice and thoughts for me. Hold me close and let me hear Your heartbeat for me. Amen"

LET'S BEGIN

"We are what we believe"
– C.S. Lewis

In the previous segment of this program, you had the courage to meet up with your younger self, this may not have been easy for you as painful memories may have surfaced, or for some it might have been a pleasant walk down memory lane as you remembered that young child in all his/her innocent cuteness.

In this module, we are going to explore how those experiences you had as baby, child or teen created a core belief in you.

You might ask what is a core belief?

A core belief is a deep rooted, automatic belief you have about yourself, about other people and the world you live in. These beliefs are absolute truths deep inside you, underneath all the thoughts that are surface.

Core beliefs are very convincing and full of persuasion, something that you accept as truth without question. Your mind filters and interprets the world, situations and circumstances through this deep root effortlessly. When something happens, your mind automatically opens the door to the core belief and consults with it for advice, safety, approval, acceptance.

A core belief becomes how you see yourself, and to what degree you feel your importance is in this world, how worthy you believe you are of love, how safe, competent, powerful and accepted you feel. Your self-esteem is rooted in that belief, and how you perceive and believe God sees you and loves you, His beautiful daughter.

Our experiences in life create an internal story in us that we tell over and over again and look to the world around us to confirm its truth.

When the story that has been created in us is positive, such as your parents telling you every day how beautiful you are, you are going to grow up with the belief that you are beautiful and valuable. If you grew up never hearing the words ' I love you' you may grow up with the belief that you are unlovable or unworthy to be loved.

A belief can come from childhood experiences, friendships, relationships, school years, jobs, experiences that we perceive as failures or accomplishments. There are many places that your beliefs become deeply rooted and through the years the story you told yourself confirmed the belief over and over again. Consider where the story may have come from. Are you hearing the voice of a parent from your childhood? Are you hearing echoes of a partner who pulled you down and undermined your self-esteem? In finding the origins of your core beliefs you will begin to challenge them and to change them.

Dr. Daniel Amen expressed:

"Your brain is always listening and responding to these hidden influences and unless you recognize and deal with them they can steal your happiness spoil your relationships and sabotage your health."

Your core beliefs have a huge influence on your sense of belonging and how you perceive others view you and are treated by others.

A negative belief about yourself is destructive to your self-acceptance and self-esteem. It is like this core belief has a voice all of its own and speaks whenever it wills.

"Beliefs have the power to create and the power to destroy. Human beings have the awesome ability to take any experience of their lives and create a meaning that dis-empowers them or one that can literally save their lives."
— Tony Robbins

Most of us will battle at some point in our lives with thoughts and feelings which threaten to derail our success and happiness. Thoughts that will keep you feeling like you cannot move forward in life and will hold you back from owning who you are and who God created you to be.

An internal judge sabotages your ability to move towards your truth and happiness. It keeps you from having compassion and gentleness with yourself.

To change the story, you are telling yourself you must first identify the belief that is limiting you and **replace it with the truth. The truth your Heavenly Father has given you and speaks over you.**

You get to rewrite your story and grasp onto beliefs that are your truth. The truths that Jesus whispers to you and writes over your life. **You are the author of your story** and the architect of your life experiences.

Are you ready to explore and debunk those negative core beliefs and fire the inner critic? Make a list of the areas in your life where you feel challenged and unhappy. Areas that you feel pressure or stuck and are not satisfied with.

What are your goals and activities you would like to do, but find a reason why you cannot do it?

Fill in the Blank
I would like to _____,
but I cannot because _____
_____

Can you identify the belief in the above statement?

I would like a relationship, a career but I cannot because _____
_____
_____

Your behavior is an indicator of your beliefs. We do not do something because we have a limited belief.

LET'S DIG DEEPER

Limited beliefs are often preceded by a fear.

Examples of fear:
- Fear of what others will think of me
- Fear of failure
- Fear of conflict

What do you fear the most? Take some time to reflect on the answer to this question.

Another way to discover fear is asking yourself "What door would I walk through if I did not fear?"

If I did not fear _____,
I would do _____
_____

Fears and limiting beliefs walk hand in hand.

There are layers of beliefs within a thought that causes your system to create fear; there is an event or a trigger, followed by a space in which we attach to a feeling of fear that immediately attaches to a belief. This belief increases the fear and the dragons in your mind have a party while they watch you hold back from being your authentic God-given self and go after the dreams and goals that you have.

Let's identify the beliefs that are holding you back - As you look at the door that fear is holding you back from, what is the belief that keeps you from opening the door and walking through it?

Chapter 3 | Belief Debunker – Redesign Your Thoughts

EXPLORING

What is the inner judge or dragon saying to you as you consider moving towards the door?

Which beliefs are having the greatest **negative** impact on your life?

With compassion and kindness examine the belief(s) and consider the change that your life would experience if you weren't held back by that belief or if that belief were eliminated from your life. What do the beliefs hold you back from?

"The only thing that's keeping you from getting what you want is the story you keep telling yourself." –Tony Robbins

Dr Caroline Leaf says:

"Whatever you think about the most will grow; if you are thinking about something daily, within approximately two months your brain has changed to accommodate this pattern of thought."

You create a filter or mindset through which you see life when you think about a situation constantly. You condition your mind to think a certain way. Similar to that of working out in the gym. When we work a certain muscle repeatedly it conditions your body to look a certain way, the same holds true for our minds, we condition them to filter our thoughts and beliefs through a negative or positive filter.

"If you realized how powerful your thoughts are, you would never think a negative thought." - Caroline Leaf

These beliefs affect our body, soul and mind.

Do your beliefs today make you question who you are? What God says about you? Your judgments? Your gut instincts? Your career? Ever feel like a fraud? Shame? Guilt? Not good enough? It is as if a dragon is sitting on your shoulder and shouting, "no see, you can't do this, you are too this and too that".

Is this your truth? Or is this a story you adopted as yours? What is truth whispering to you? **What is the truth wanting to say to you?** What is Papa God saying to you? What does He say your truth is?

Ask me and I will tell you remarkable secrets you do not know about things to come. - Jeremiah 33:3 NLT

Let Him tell you these secrets about you. It is in Him that your identity is grounded in truth and in love.

Ask Him, Papa what is your truth about me? Who does He say you are? **Journal what you hear from Him.**

Are you going to give the dragon power or the truth? **It is your choice.**

Our beliefs about ourselves will propel us forward or hold us back. **They shape the decisions we make**, our yes and our no, our boundaries and the way we communicate. Our energy and the way we see ourselves and the way we believe God sees us which affects the way we receive love from Him.

We all have names, beliefs, lies, words we have believed. Beliefs that create a shame and/or fear within us.

Can you see we all have insecurities? We compare, we put ourselves down, we criticize ourselves and others due to our insecurities. What would it feel like to view yourself as equal to the person you so admire?

After all God is not partial, He creates each of us equal, so why can we not see ourselves as equal, why do we tear ourselves down? Let's look at a couple scriptures that express equality.

There is neither Jew nor Greek, there is neither slave nor free, there is no male and female, for you are all one in Christ Jesus. – Galatians 3:28

For God shows no partiality. - Romans 2:11

Truly, truly, I say to you, a servant is not greater than his master, nor is a messenger greater than the one who sent him. - John 13:16

So God created man in his own image, in the image of God he created him; male and female he created them. - Genesis 1:27

Most of us will battle at some point in our lives with thoughts and feelings which threaten to derail our success, happiness and joy.

Do you celebrate your victories or focus on your failures? Do you look truthfully at what you are doing in your own life and what others are doing? Do you thank God for creating you to be the unique woman He made you?

Chapter 3 | Belief Debunker – Redesign Your Thoughts

The comedian Irwin Corey once remarked that

"If we don't change direction soon, we will end up where we're going."

By **identifying and changing** the core beliefs in our mind so many of our uncomfortable emotions and sabotaging behaviors dissolve away. The first two and most critical steps in this process are to **invite Jesus into each belief and to be aware and listen for who He says you are.**

JOURNALING

Write a word blast, uncensored, any and all thoughts that are in your mind. Write about the dreams and goals you have and let the thoughts form words on paper read what you wrote, and observe the words with curiosity. Are they positive or negative? What beliefs about yourself can you identify in your words?

In the narrative of these thoughts, you create a story about yourselves. Do you recognize a judge in your story? Is there a victim voice (poor me) (helpless) a voice that accepts and takes on the voice of the judge? A voice that accepts the voice of the judge to be true? Do you base your identity on what the judge and victim are saying? Is there a persecutor voice that is harsh?

Here are some other examples of common core beliefs that we hide inside:
- I am irredeemably flawed.
- Something is wrong with me
- I am unlovable.
- I am bad.
- I am stupid.
- I am worthless.
- I am a loser.
- I don't deserve good things.
- I am a failure.
- I am weak.
- I am not enough.
- I don't matter.
- I am bored.
- I am crazy and unstable.
- I can't be fixed.
- I always hurt people
- I always hurt myself.
- I have no hope.
- I am bad
- I am unwanted.
- I am invisible.
- I made a mistake.
- I am helpless.
- I am ugly.
- I am shameful.
- I am uninteresting.
- I will die alone.

DEBUNKING THE BELIEF

Often, you'll discover that there is one main core belief that seems to pervade a lot of what you think, feel and do. Challenge and debunk this belief first. The thoughts that we suppress hurt us. **Bring it out into the open as if you are going into battle with your dragon. Challenge it. Correct it!**

Write down your negative core belief (the act of writing it down gives it less power) You may have more than one belief that you want to work through this process with.

Is it true? On a scale of 1 to 10, how much do you truly believe this belief? *Rate how much conviction you have in your core belief.*

I Don't Believe At All   Strongly Believe

1_____5_____10

Ask yourself, "Why do I believe this is true about myself?"

Is it 100% true?

How do I feel when I believe this thought?

Reflect on memories or experiences that hold your belief. Identify any emotions (such as fear) hiding behind your beliefs.

How would I feel if I didn't have this thought?

What does God say about this belief?

EXPLORE HIDDEN FORMS OF RESISTANCE

You will need to be able to deeply commit to the journey of rewriting limiting beliefs, by becoming conscious of what is holding you back from changing

Is this belief serving you today? When you can see that you are no longer being positively served by this deeply held conviction it is easier to make room for new and positive beliefs. What has long lasting (eternal) value? Am I acting in a way that will make me proud of my life? In a way that makes God smile?

By managing thoughts and creating a thought routine we can debunk and redesign the thought.

1. Take the original thought, turn it to the opposite, flip it. It's important that you choose a core belief that you genuinely believe in.

2. Is this new belief true?

3. What is the evidence of truth for this new opposite thought?

4. Ask Papa God, what is the truth? What do You want to say to me? He is waiting and longing to tell you the truth about who you are

5. Examine the cost and the benefit of the new belief.

6. Create 2 lists. One list is the costs of having the new belief and one listing the benefits you will gain with the new belief.

7. Again…What is your truth?

8. What is the evidence of the truth for this new opposite thought?

9. Explore how your life will change with your new truth and belief.

10. How will your new core belief transform your life? Will it help you to be more joyful, confident, creative or prosperous?

11. Is this new belief in alignment with God's truth for you?

12. If you don't change your core beliefs, what will be the consequence?

13. Reflect on or write down your thoughts.

14. What is the evidence of truth for this new opposite thought?

15. What action steps can you put into place to ensure the truth becomes an automatic belief that replaces the limiting belief.

Whenever you experience a **ebb and flown i**n emotion, pay attention!

Replacing your core beliefs will take time and effort, but the rewards are endless and priceless. Increased self-esteem, creativity, productivity, prosperity, joy, fulfillment, and love are some of the many gifts you will receive throughout this journey of rewriting your internal dialogue and story.

Look at it as **washing your brain clean**. We wash our bodies, hands ,hair, why wouldn't we wash our brains of toxic, negative thinking **so we have clean thinking.**

Jesus longs to wash your mind of negative beliefs and show you a new way of thinking. He is a change-maker and way maker. Spending intentional time in His word and with Him will purposefully change the negative beliefs to thinking that will forever change your life. He wants to lavish His love on you in a way that erases the old and brings a delight and excitement to your soul.

COACH VS JUDGE

If you think of a little child, their 'look mom look, see what I did' ' they are always looking for the coach... you are born with an inner coach that encourages and looks for the successes, over the years this voice was told to be quiet, and the judge stepped in.

Claim back and strengthen your inner greatness and coach by giving it permission to look for the truth in each thought.

Write down all your successes, your proud moments, your accomplishments. Rejoice in them, cherish them. Invite 'Jesus' to show you and remind you of these accomplishments.

For each fear write an act of courage or accomplishment in your life

For each limiting belief write your truth,

FOOD FOR THOUGHT

Scientifically we have 90 seconds from the time a thought enters your mind to either hock into it or to let it pass by. You get to choose whether you hook into a limiting thought or a positive thought and to tell the limiting or negative thought that you do not have space for negativity or limits and to leave.

ADDITIONAL EXERCISE – *WHO DOES GOD SAY YOU ARE?*

Search the scriptures for all the names He calls you. This exercise can be done by sitting with your Bible and searching or doing a google search. Don't quit at 2 or 3 names, keep going until you feel the words resonate over you with an awe.

SELF-CARE

Create a playlist of all your favorite worship and other music that motivates and inspires you. Listen to these songs, listen to the lyrics and let yourself feel His love flow over you as He whispers His love for you.

Go for a walk, inviting Jesus to walk with you and show you His love as you walk together. Spend time each day with Jesus. Create space to just be with Him. He delights in spending time with you, His daughter.

HOMEWORK FOR THIS WEEK

Picture yourself living life in your truth. What does this look like? What are you doing?

Do something that has scared you to do because you believed the judge and dragon. Journal the above exercise and how you felt doing it

MY PRAYER FOR YOU TODAY

"Papa, You see this beautiful woman, your daughter, you know that pain she has walked through and the negative beliefs she has believed, the lies that the enemy put in front of her to believe. Papa saturates her with your truths, let her see how you see her. Let the truth be planted deep in her soul and in her mind. Let her know her beauty, because in that place, with your truth she is unstoppable, Amen"

CHAPTER FOUR
ARCHITECT OF YOUR STORY

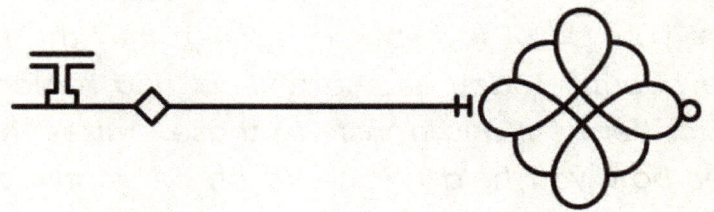

GROUNDING EXERCISE

Find a space to relax and get comfortable - put some soaking **worship music on to still your heart, mind and soul** .

- Pause
- Close your eyes
- Picture a peaceful place, either in real life or an imaginary place in your mind.
- Invite Jesus into the picture... Where is He? *(holding you, dancing with you, carrying you or walking to meet you?)*
- Take five deep breaths *(with each inhale, breath in the peace, with each exhale, picture the stresses of the day leaving your body)*
- Focus on your 4 senses, one at a time
    - What do I feel?
    - What do you see?
    - What do I smell?
    - What do I hear?

Notice how you feel after you have completed this grounding exercise. Notice the muscle tension, has it been released? This breathing exercise is meant to ground you in preparation for today's module.

SONG OF THE DAY

Prepare your heart for more by listening to the suggested worship music. **Below is a song by Casting Crowns that has been chosen for you. Be still and let the music and words speak to you.**

[Casting Crowns - The Change In Me](#)

PRAYER

"Heavenly Father, write your story on this beautiful woman's heart. Where there is pain, let her feel your oil of love begin to seep into the pain and transform her story from ashes into beauty. Today as she reflects and remembers, dance with her, let her feel your love for her heal and transform those bruises that have been placed on her heart. Let her see how you hold her heart, oh so gently and with unconditional love that is hard for her to fathom. Amen."

LET'S BEGIN

This segment of the course is short but thought provoking. My hope for you is that in this time you will gain a deeper understanding of yourself and your story and how Jesus takes the pieces of our stories and creates a beautiful tapestry from them.

Our stories do help to shape us, but they do not need to define us unless we so often let them.

I am going to share a little piece of my personal journey in discovering acceptance for myself and for my story.

I hated me and I hated my story!

I was great at hiding. Hiding my true self under a pretense of quiet and shy. I was scared to be seen and to be heard. I was ashamed of who I was and where I came from.

I sat one day with a coach, he had an assignment for me that I resented and felt like it was a complete waste of my time… But…it had a profound effect on how I viewed my story.

He said " I want you to write a letter to your 18 year old self the night before you got married" and " remember, you had a choice".

My letter was formulated in my head in a bunker, and later put on paper. I was working at a golf course at 5:30 AM. In the stillness of the morning, while raking bunkers, I found it was a great time for some deep reflecting and soul searching.

That day, in the bunker, my story changed, it no longer has the power to control me or define me, but I came to the deep realization that my story shaped me and continues to shape who I am today and my future.

You see, I was letting my story create negative beliefs in me about who I am and what my value was based on what happened to me and around me, I believed lies about myself that led me to believe that I was unlovable, unworthy, unimportant and so many other negative beliefs. This also led me to believe that my Heavenly Father made a mistake when He made me and didn't love me very much at all. Logically I had a knowing 'oh ya, God loves me' but in my heart, I could not accept I was worthy of love.

Your story also shapes you. You have a choice at how you write your story.

You have an opportunity to rewrite your stories and the narrative you have believed. What would it be like to change the narrative you tell yourself and at the same time come to a deeper knowing of the crazy "madly in love' your Heavenly Papa has for you.

Before you go into letter writing, take some time to reflect on the exercise below:

TIMELINE
On a blank paper draw a timeline.

Date of Birth   Present Time
(0 months) _____ (current age)

For every event that is memorable to you, mark it on the timeline. For every sad or painful event make a line downward and for every happy and positive event make a line upwards. The length of the mark will be determined by the depth / impact of the event. Example - the day you got married may be a long line upwards. The day you lost a job would be a line down. The day you lost someone you love is a longer line downward. The greater the loss the longer the line.

Look at the up and down lines as your heartbeat on a heart monitor. It is your story, your pain, your joy, it is what you have experienced.

Reflect on your timeline. How does it make you feel to look at the timeline that tells a snapshot story about you?

Invite Jesus into the timeline. Ask where He was in the painful moments and in the joy filled moments. It may sound like this:

"Jesus where were you when _____.
Show me where you were in that moment when I was hurting so much."

Be still and let Him show you, sometimes He speaks in pictures, scripture, song or word. Let Him into the space. Journal what He brings to you.

DEAR YOUNGER ME

Listen to the song **suggestion by Nichole Nordeman** below before you begin this segment.

Nichole Nordeman – Dear Me

Create some time in your schedule. Find a place that is quiet and undisturbed.

Write a letter to your younger self at a pivotal point in your life.

Picture your younger self today, go for a walk with her, where you loved to go when you were young.

I found myself sitting on my bed in my childhood home with my young teen self. As I pictured myself sitting there, my heart softened, and I became compassionate for the young version of me.

Picture your younger self... what would the adult you say to the younger you.

Dear 5-year-old me....
Dear 10-year-old ....(insert name here)
Dear 15-year-old....

You may choose to write to different ages of this young and beautiful/handsome girl/boy.

Remember in life we have a choice, even when we do not feel like we do, it may be as drastic as choosing life over death. It may be the most tragic and painful moment but you chose life, you are here today, lovely and beautiful in who you are.

Dear_____,

REFLECTION

How did writing this letter affect you?

What new insight did you gain?

How does it shift your perception of your story?

How does it shift the story you tell yourself about your value and worth?

Invite and ask Jesus where He was/is in your story.

Can you begin to see the 'beauty for ashes?

I like God's promise to us in the following verses:

*"...For I will turn their mourning into joy
And will comfort them and give them joy for their sorrow."* - Jeremiah 31:13b

"Now may the God of hope fill you with all joy and peace in believing, so that you will abound in hope by the power of the Holy Spirit." - Romans 15:13

JOURNALING

How can your story be used to impact others and help make the world a better place?

What are the unique gifts and qualities that have become a part of you through your story?

What desires and dreams have grown?

If you met another woman at the coffee shop, and over a cup of spicy latte, she shared a story with you that was like your story, how would you see her? What compassion would you have for her? What would you say to her as she shares? And as she sits back in her chair with a deep sigh and a tear in her eye and says "and that is how I got here today" what would you look at her and say?

Would you look at her and say words that were harsh and judgmental, or would you gently touch her hand with compassion and say 'wow, thank you for sharing, you are incredible and strong, courageous for having come through all that and be sitting here today. Your story is inspiring.'

Reflect on this question and journal your answer. A beautiful woman sits across the table from you and tells you her story, which is yours. What do you say to her? What do you say to you?

You are designed and created for greatness.

Like the oyster that takes sand from the bottom of the ocean, and then becomes a pearl, this too, is what your story, all the pain, hurt, tragedy and glorious moments have created in you. A beautiful pearl!

Your endurance, your courage. YOU! YES YOU, have an incredible story that has helped to shape you into the glorious person that you are today, and God has a purpose for you and your story, He takes the pieces, holds them gently in His hands and whispers His love over them. The pieces that you feel are so broken and wasted, He takes them and wants you to know how precious and beautiful they are to Him.

Let the words of the **following song by Bethel Music** flow through you.

[Bethel Music – Dancing on the Waves](#)

SELF-CARE

Take time this week to go for a walk. Get into nature and enjoy the beauty around you. Be aware of your senses as you walk, the smells, sounds and sights.

Do something for you - it may be eating an ice cream cone or going for a kayak ride or just sitting in the sun, whatever it is, do something that brings you joy in your soul.

HOMEWORK

Reread the letter you wrote to your younger self. Reflect some more on the strengths and beauty that have been instilled deep in your soul from the journey you have been on. Spend time here reflecting and letting the truth of your journey soak into your heart.

MY PRAYER FOR YOU TODAY

"Papa, remembering is not always easy, today this beautiful woman has remembered joyful moments and times filled with pain and tears. Comfort her as she remembers and heals. Let your oil of healing and love flow over her from the top of her head to the tip of her toes. I pray Papa, that she will feel your love in a new and refreshing way, that she will see how you love to take those broken pieces and put them together in a new and refined way. That you take her mourning and turn it to joy, the ashes of her pain and turn it to beauty, this is your specialty. I pray that her heart will be filled with hope and peace, knowing you are holding her every step of the way. Continue to heal her heart and mind throughout this week. Show her Your love in crazy and amazing ways, that she just knows it is You."

CHAPTER FIVE
POWER IN FORGIVENESS

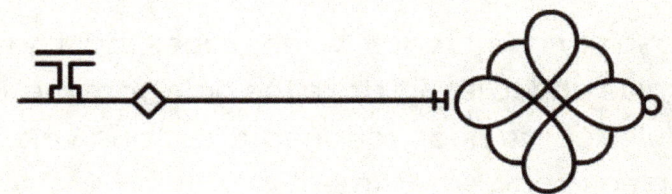

GROUNDING EXERCISE

Find a space to relax and get comfortable - put some soaking worship music on to quiet your heart and mind in preperation for this next segment.

- Pause
- Close your eyes
- Picture a peaceful place, either in real life or an imaginary place in your mind.
- Invite Jesus into the picture... Where is He? *(holding you, dancing with you, carrying you or walking to meet you?)*
- Take five deep breaths *(with each inhale, breath in the peace, with each exhale, picture the stresses of the day leaving your body)*
- Focus on your 4 senses, one at a time
    - What do I feel?
    - What do you see?
    - What do I smell?
    - What do I hear?

Notice how you feel after you have completed this grounding exercise. Notice the muscle tension, has it been released? This breathing exercise is meant to ground you in preparation for today's module.

SONG OF THE DAY

Music chosen for today's module. Listen to the words and let the music prepare your heart for letting go. **Music suggestion by Fearless Soul and Hillsong Young & Free**

1. [Fearless Soul](#)
2. [Hillsong Young & Free - Letting Go](#)

PRAYER

"Papa, open my heart today to the places that I have locked up that you want to heal. Help me to forgive and to let You take the pain from me. Hold me close to You as we walk through this module, let me hear Your heartbeat and when I feel too scared or hurt to keep going forward, please carry me. Amen"

Chapter 5 | Power In Forgiveness

LET'S BEGIN

Forgiveness is at the core of healing. When you forgive, it sets you free and allows your heart to heal, opening doors to endless possibilities.

Forgiveness is not easy, nor is it always about forgiving someone else. Forgiving someone that has hurt you is vital to your wellbeing, but just as important is **forgiving yourself,** which I, personally, have often found to be the most difficult action. In this chapter, you may need to walk through forgiveness for more than one person.

When you forgive you are not excusing or justifying the actions of someone, but rather, you are lifting the burden from your heart.

Forgiveness stems from a deep belief **that you are enough, that you are loved** and that even though you were wronged, you don't have to spend your emotional energy trying to get revenge or have the debt paid back for the pain that was instilled on you. It takes practice to train our minds to learn the art of forgiving and letting go of what was to make room for healing and new opportunities.

Jesus took the greatest weight of the world's sin and in His deepest pain He said:

"Father, forgive them, for they do not know what they are doing." – Luke 23:34

When I stop and think of what He has forgiven me, and the example of forgiveness He gave to the world to follow, when I think of the freedom I get to experience because of His sacrifice. My heart knows that forgiving others and myself is the only way to experience the complete freedom that He has for you and me.

Healing and forgiveness walk hand in hand. **Forgive yourself, forgive others, forgive life itself and experience a freedom, wholeness and joy deep within your heart.**

Practicing forgiveness, releasing resentment and learning acceptance is an opportunity to practice love even when it's not easy. Another commandment that Jesus gives us is:

"Be kind and compassionate to one another, forgiving each other, just as in Christ God forgave you." – Ephesians 4:32

Forgiveness is a form of surrender and release, expanding our capacity to love. It is setting a prisoner free. You set yourself free when **you set others free** and when you forgive yourself.

Forgiveness is a journey, not a destination. Sometimes forgiveness happens in layers, and we need to forgive many times over. I would like to say that forgiveness is a 'once forgiven, all forgotten", however in our humanistic ways, we do not forget and often pick up the backpack of unforgiveness again, taking it with us through life, until we again choose to unpack the backpack and forgive. **It is a choice we get to make each day** - To forgive or to remain hurt.

Peter, one of Jesus' disciples asked Him:

"Lord, how many times shall I forgive my brother or sister who sins against me? Up to seven times?" and Jesus answered Peter with a reply that is thought provoking, "I tell you, not seven times, but seventy-seven times.
- Matthew 18:21-22

Oh, how those words can slice us to the core, how many times don't we cut someone off at the knees when they have wronged us, but Jesus says seventy-seven times. Or we know that the pain that was caused against us is unforgivable, but Jesus forgave even the worst of offenses. He was spat on, beaten, mocked, and hung on a cross to die, but what did He do, He forgave His abusers and the ones that killed Him.

Forgiveness does not mean that you let the individual hurt you again, or even that you let them back into your life. Forgiveness is an act of setting yourself free of the resentment, bitterness and pain caused by the wrongdoing and setting healthy boundaries for yourself.

Forgiveness is a choice and when we choose to forgive it brings transformation. It transforms us from victim to survivor, from helpless to empowered. **It brings freedom to our minds and hearts when we embrace opportunities to forgive.**

Forgiveness means finding the courage to see our own errors – not just those of others. It turns away the false messages of harsh self-judgment to ourselves and judgment to another.

When we choose to forgive it brings transformation. It transforms us from victim to survivor, from helpless to empowered. It brings freedom to our minds and hearts when we embrace opportunities to forgive.

REFLECTIONS - BLOCKS TO FORGIVING

- Do I believe that forgiving requires something of the other person first?

- Has this wrongdoing, pain and resentment become part of my identity?

- What are the pleasures of this anger and resentment?

- Is there a part of me that wants to entertain the anger?

- Is withholding forgiveness about my ego?

- What would forgiveness look like?

- Is this where I want to stay?

Reflect and journal your thoughts and emotions from the above questions.

STEPS TOWARDS FORGIVENESS

Invite Jesus into the process of forgiveness, into the pain. Ask Him if there is anything hidden/blocked that needs to be forgiven.

- **Name the wound/hurt. What caused the pain?**

- **Name the trigger.**

- **Name the person that hurt you.**

During this phase of forgiveness, you will gain a deeper understanding of the injustice, and how it has impacted your life. Begin exploring by describing the pain you have endured.

NOTE: If you are feeling retraumatized, do a grounding technique and enter the process slowly when you are ready or talk with a trained trauma counselor.

- **Remember the pain of the incident. What happened?**

- **What is the hardest thing to forgive?**

- Why was this treatment unfair? How have the injustices affected you?

- Where do you carry this in your body?

- How long have you carried the pain?

Imagine taking it from your body and holding it in your hands as if it were a ball. Look at it from every angle with compassion and curiosity.

The next questions may seem irrelevant, however please answer the questions quickly, without thinking deep into them.

- What color is it?

- What shape is it?

- Does it have a smell?

- Does it make a noise?

- How old is it?

Observe and look at the object you have described with curiosity. As you continue to process through forgiveness, you will come back to this object that you have described.

During the decision phase of forgiveness, you will gain a deeper understanding of what forgiveness is and make the decision to choose or reject forgiveness as an option.

Forgiveness is a choice you get to make.

You may wrestle with the decision to forgive because you have the right to be angry, while the offender does not have the right to kindness. Making the decision to forgive means letting go of these resentments *(which you have every right to hold)* **so you can heal**.

A lot of people hang on to unforgiveness because they are afraid that forgiving means letting the offender back into their lives, which could cause more harm. This is not so, **forgiving means you are setting yourself free**, and keeping healthy boundaries with the offender, for you this might mean never seeing the person again to keep yourself safe.

Do you want to keep the resentment, pain and unforgiveness?

Are you willing to let it go?

What are the pros and cons of deciding to forgive the person who wronged you?

Pros:

Cons:

Describe how things might be different if you decide to forgive.

OBSERVE

During the process of **letting go** you may start to observe and understand the offender in a new way, which will allow new feelings toward the offender and yourself. Learning to understand the offender, and to see them as more than their wrongdoing, is an important part of forgiveness. However, **it is vital for you to understand** that this does not mean condoning the act that caused harm. You can gain understanding and compassion for another person without believing their actions are acceptable.

Observe the object in your hands from the other person's point of view.

- Does it look the same from his/her view?

- Let's look at it from another angle

- What was life like for this person as they were growing up?

- May this have impacted their behavior?

- What was life like for this person at the time of the offense?

- What feelings do you currently have toward the offender?

Journal your thoughts and emotions as you look at each of the above questions?

Observe the painful object in your hands from the point of view of a bystander, someone with an unbiased view. I like to refer to this as the helicopter view. Someone with an unobstructive point of view.

JOURNAL YOUR OBSERVATION

During the deepening stage of forgiveness, you may find meaning in the experiences, and recognize ways in which you have grown as a result.

Take some time to breathe deep as you notice the emotions you may be experiencing.

Invite Jesus to go deeper with you as you process and observe the emotions you are feeling.

Who is the hardest person to forgive?

What is it you want to hold onto?

Have you held onto the pain for long enough now that it might be safe to let it go?

What benefit is there in forgiving?

Could you give understanding to yourself and to the other person? Compassion? Acceptance? Can you forgive and release?

Would you be willing to change the belief that you are deserving of the pain to a belief that you are worthy of being loved, protected and cherished?

How willing are you to let go and release, in order to gain the freedom that forgiveness brings?

Release all the pain.
All the bitterness.
Release the person - let him/her go.
Set them free.

For an audio version of a Forgiveness Journey, copy the following link into your browser.

https://youtu.be/NH_9h3NQ6Cg

By setting them free you are setting yourself free.

Say to him/her "I forgive you for not being the way I wanted and needed you to be. I set you free. I set the experience of pain free"

Observe the object in your hand from the above exercise. Has it changed shape or color?

Decide - do you want to let it go completely?

When you feel ready say the following statements out loud to yourself.

"I forgive _____ and set you free. I forgive myself and set myself free. I am forgiven, and I am free"

Spend some time in prayer and ask Jesus if there is anything else that He wants to bring to mind to forgive, either someone that has caused you pain, or an unforgiveness for yourself that you might still be holding onto.

Consider how forgiveness has affected your emotional health, behavioral changes that resulted from the injustice, and time/energy spent thinking about the offender.

Describe how you have grown because of the pain you endured and your efforts to forgive. How has your worldview changed?

Are you stronger than you were before deciding to forgive?

What has changed for you during the forgiveness process?

Forgiving is not easy and many times it is a journey that **we need to choose to repeat over and over again** until it does not hold the same bitterness, resentment or fear.

You took a courageous and painful journey today. A journey that is vital to your freedom and growth. Unforgiveness is relentless in holding us in a stuck pattern of believing we are victims and not worthy of more in life.

You are worthy and deserving of a life full of joy and freedom.

LISTENING PRAYER

There is no greater Healer of hearts than our Master Healer, Jesus. In His time on earth, He created many miracles of healing...and today He still heals. He wants nothing more than to heal the brokenness in your heart, to wipe your tears and make your sorrow turn to laughter and dancing.

Take some time now to be still and listen.

Ask Jesus – What do you want to say to me?

Be specific – What do you want to say to me about the person that hurt me?

What do you want to say to me about my hurt?

Jesus, how do you see me?

How do you love me?

Let His whisper of love, His words wash over you. He may speak to you through a song, a word, a verse, a picture, or you may hear a quietness in your heart that knows the words that come to mind are Jesus words to you.

JOURNALING

Journal what you hear and what comes to mind from your time in listening prayer. This quiet time with Papa, may be something you come back to in the future to be reminded of His love and promises to you.

SELF-CARE

Rest - you have been on a journey, and it is time to rest. This may be a hot bath or a stroll in the park or forest. Take time to sit and just breathe, noticing each breath you take, as a gift of life.

HOMEWORK

Write a letter of forgiveness to the person that caused you pain. Tell them about the pain you endured and tell them you forgive them, and that you are no longer holding him/her hostage in your mind/ heart anymore. There's power in the act of writing the words. You may choose to give the letter OR you may choose to keep it for a reminder to yourself of the process you walked through

MY PRAYER FOR YOU TODAY

"Papa, thank you for forgiving each of us and for being an example for us to follow. I pray today for this courageous woman to feel the release and freedom that forgiveness brings. I pray for her heart to feel the lightness, freedom, peace and joy that You have for her. Continue to bring her a sense of Your nearness as she walks in her new freedom, free of the burden of unforgiveness. I pray that she will continue to see herself as You see her, your beautiful daughter and the memories of the past can be washed away and exchanged for a memory of your love for her. Amen."

CHAPTER SIX

DESIGNING YOUR ROAD MAP

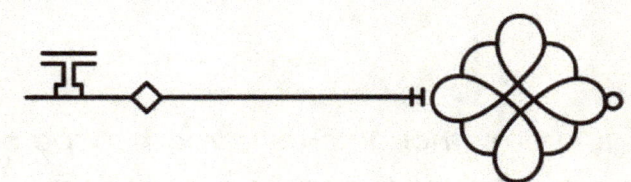

GROUNDING EXERCISE

Find a space to relax and get comfortable - put some soaking music **to still your heart and soul and to set your heart to hear His heart beat for you.**

- Pause
- Close your eyes
- Picture a peaceful place, either in real life or an imaginary place in your mind.
- Invite Jesus into the picture... Where is He? *(holding you, dancing with you, carrying you or walking to meet you?)*
- Take five deep breaths *(with each inhale, breath in the peace, with each exhale, picture the stresses of the day leaving your body)*
- Focus on your 4 senses, one at a time
    - What do I feel?
    - What do you see?
    - What do I smell?
    - What do I hear?

Notice how you feel after you have completed this grounding exercise. Notice the muscle tension, has it been released? This breathing exercise is meant to ground you in preparation for today's module.

Prepare your heart for more by listening to music. Below is a song that has been chosen for you. Be still and let the music and words speak to you.

SONG OF THE DAY

Music suggestion for today **by Hillsong Young & Free and Anthem Lights** ~ Let the words guide your heart in preparation for discovering more about your beautiful and amazing self.

1. [Hillsong Young and Free - Wake](#)
2. [Anthem Lights – Who I'm Meant To Be](#)

PRAYER

"Papa, guide my thoughts as I dream, hope and plan. Show me Your dreams for me. For us. Guide my thoughts and be my wisdom. Plan for my future with me and reveal to me what you want me to do next. Show me your heart for me. Amen"

LET'S BEGIN

If you had unlimited resources and couldn't fail, **if you had no fear, what would you set out to do?**

If you had all the confidence you want, and a complete knowing that God is with you in every situation, what would you dare to do?

Setting goals for your life provides direction and is a motivator. Without goals it is difficult to focus and to achieve the dreams you have. It is like a ship at sea without a compass. Or driving through a new country without a roadmap to guide you. **Without a target to aim for, you cannot hit the destination,** so it is important to have goals that are specific, measurable, attainable and action orientated. A goal is an idea or a desired result that you have for your life, a destination you would like to reach.

"A dream is your creative vision for your life in the future. A goal is what specifically you intend to happen. Dreams and goals should be just out of your present reach but not out of sight. Dreams and goals are coming attractions in your life" - Joseph Campbell

What are some of your dreams for your life?

What if for this one day only, anything you dream will come out good - there is no way you can fail. What would you dare to dream if this were true?

It can feel overwhelming to begin with or you may have ideas but feel overwhelmed with actually attaining them.

Lets look at this verse for a moment:

"For I know the plans I have for you," declares the Lord, "plans to prosper and not to harm you, plans to give you hope and a future". - Jeremiah 29:11 NIV

God invites you to partner with Him for your future. He has put dreams, creative ideas and hopes into you for a reason. He has gifted you with qualities and characteristics to carry out His dreams for you. He wants to be invited into your dreams and plans.

Spend time with Jesus, soak in His presence. The more time you spend with Him, the easier it is to recognize His voice and the direction He gives. A verse I love, that shows His heart for us as His kids and His desire for us to come to Him with our questions, dreams and just whatever is on our hearts:

"Ask me and I will tell you remarkable secrets you do not know about things to come." - Jeremiah 33:3 NLT

LIFE INVENTORY

The ladder of life of life is a first step to defining changes you want to make in your life and to begin setting goals. You completed a life inventory in the introduction of this course to raise your awareness and to reflect on where you are at. **This** ladder is intended for you to examine close up where you are and where you want to be. Without knowing where you desire to be, you will be like a ship at sea with no rudder, tossed to and fro in the wind. Having a direction to work towards is the light guiding you.

Label the sections of the ladder with the categories that are most significant to you.

- Family
- Personal growth
- Self-care
- Exercise/fitness
- Love/Romance
- Friendship
- Finance/Money
- Career/Business
- Health
- Community
- Spirituality
- Housing

The bottom of the ladder of life represents 0% satisfaction and fulfillment in this area of your life and the top of the ladder represents 100% satisfied and fulfilled. Spend some time putting thought and reflection into this process to create the most accurate picture of your life balance and satisfaction. After you place all of your categories, sit back and reflect on the inventory before you. Are you satisfied with each category? Are there changes you would like to see in the categories?

Chapter 6 | Designing Your Road Map

Picture the ladder as if it was placed in position, leaning against a cloud marked "goals / dreams". As you look at how far up you have climbed in each category, does the category help you reach your goals and dreams? Or is it hindering your climb? What areas would you like to make changes to in order to create more balance and fulfillment in your life? This exercise can feel discouraging when you are not experiencing fullness and balance, but to be very clear, this is not meant for you to beat yourself up but rather to bring **awareness, hope and clarity.**

What we do not know, we cannot change!

Defining the changes that you want to make - your goals and destination is something that takes thought and time. But **without action steps the goal will remain a dream**. It takes beginning with the end in mind and a clear understanding of your destination and where you're going so that you have your compass pointed in the right direction at all times. A focus point to aim for.

Tony Robbins expresses it this way:

"You can't have a plan for your day, until you have a plan for your life."

A lot of people dream and plan with limitations of their own belief systems. What if you dared to dream and think with the potential of a lifetime? **What if you dared to dream as a King's daughter?** Remember you are His beloved daughter, and He has great and wondrous plans for your life.

What if for a moment you let your imagination go and visualized a life without limitations and rather looked at the potential that lies within you. The greatness that you have been unlocking for the past few weeks that is begging to be let free.

What if you dared to dream in terms of your God-given potential instead of your current capabilities and the limited belief you have about your circumstances. How would it change your dream and how you perceive your capabilities?

Chapter 6 | Designing Your Road Map

REFLECTION

"Miracle Question. The following question is a thought-provoking question. Take some time to let yourself explore your dreams and what lies within you.

Imagine that tonight as you sleep a miracle occurs in your life. A magical momentous happening that has completely solved your problems and rippled out to cover and infinitely improve all areas of your life. Your life is exactly like you want it to be. Your career, relationships, where you live.

***Think for a moment and tell me... how is life different when you wake up and go about your day? What's the first thing you'll notice as you wake up in the morning?* "**
(Used in solution focused therapy created by Insoo Kim Berg & Steven de Shazer)

Describe your day/life in detail.

Now that you have the creativity and vision flowing...

Take 10 minutes to do a brain dump of all of your dreams, goals, aspirations, things you would like to do and achieve and experiences that you would like to have. Hold nothing back, big and small, there is no wrong answer. Write as fast as you can and **give yourself permission to dream big with Papa. He has dreams for you.**

Imagine Jesus sitting with you and listing off His dreams for you. Add them all to your brain dump. There are no right or wrong answers for this exercise.

What do you really want to do with your life? What would you like to accomplish with your life?

What would you regret not doing if you suddenly found you had a limited amount of time left on the earth?

Brain Dump:

GOALS TIMELINE

Create a timeline. *(I found the simplest way of doing this and a good visualization was to tape paper to a wall in a room)*

Begin with the big picture - take the words from the brain dump list, that you want to accomplish in 10 years, another paper labeled 5 years, 4 years and so on until you reach 1 year. This can be career, finances, business, relationships, travel, education, ect. When you reach 1 year, break it down into months until you reach 1 month from today's date.

Be realistic with your times, make them achievable timelines so as not to lose momentum.

Take a step back and reflect on your work. How does it feel to see your dreams as a road map in front of you? It may be overwhelming, hopeful, invigorating.

Is there anything you want to add or take away?

Review your work and break this into smaller steps.

What action steps do you need to take in order to reach each goal?

What action steps do you need to take this week to reach your goal for 1 month from now?

Write these action steps on a schedule so that you have definite dates on which to do things. Your action steps will be what moves you forward and makes that goal a reality. Make them simple, have an accountability partner, tackle them in order of importance.

Take your top 5 goals and write a description for each goal explaining why it is important for you to reach this goal. Why it excites you.

1.

2.

3.

4.

5.

Say the goal out loud to yourself, share it with a trusted friend. Speaking it out loud creates a reality and a determination. Let it sink in.

At the end of each month/ year, review what you have completed, mark things off the checklists for each step taken and goal achieved. Write up the schedule with the action points you need for the next year.

Celebrate each goal that you reach. It is important to acknowledge your achievements. Be proud of yourself for the accomplishments.

Your goals can transform your life in ways that help you unlock the extraordinary in you!

Does your goal align with God's heart for you? Do you experience a calm, a peace and an excitement? Where there is an unrest or unsettled feeling in your soul, this is an opportunity to ask God "am I in alignment with you|?

Not all unrest is out of alignment, sometimes it is a fear of the unknown or fear of a new task that seems scary and too big. Remember, God will never call you too something that He is not equipping you for and that you cannot accomplish, but He will stretch you, because He knows what He has created you for and what He has put inside you. **He will call you into much bigger things than what you think you are capable of**. When the task before you seems daunting and scary, **He is asking you to trust Him.**

Lean into the amazing journey He wants to take you on and remember that **He equips you for what He calls you to.** His dreams for you are so big and beautiful, more than what you can imagine, that **you have no choice but to lean into Him, and that is what He desires for you, a co-relationship with Him** as you go after the dreams He has planted in your heart.

Here's a question to ponder… Is it more painful to keep all your hopes, dreams, goals, desires locked up inside of you or get them out there into the world, pursue them, and possibly fail but know you gave it everything and experienced the journey?

Keep your heart open. Be observant to when you are at your happiest, healthiest, and most energized. God and life have a way of telling you when you need to step into another goal, or that a goal no longer fits for who you are and where you are at.

Review what limitations or obstacles might come in your way of achieving your destination?

What do you need to put into place to remove and/or support you through these obstacles?

Imagine you are 90 years old, sitting on your front porch and looking back at your life, which dream from your list would cause the greatest regret if you had NOT pursued it? What is the cost of not pursuing it? What Is the benefit? How will your life look different if you pursue and accomplish your dream? How will it look if you do not?

Reaching Your goals is not an easy journey. **It takes perseverance, dedication, a lot of courage and stepping outside your comfort zone**. But the more you practice using these tools for the journey, the stronger you become…until one day it is more uncomfortable to NOT step into the courage, the dreams God gave you and move forward, than it is to stay in the comfort zone and not achieve your goals.

Goals big and small can be the stepping-stones to a fulfilled, passionate life that you get to create.

'In the end, the overriding factor is whether or not you realize your dreams are going to be you. Not the world. YOU.' – Russel Simmons

You are going to be the moving force behind the achievement of your dreams. You will be the one to stop or go. When God says go, we do have a choice to make, do we step forward with courage and faith, **into the greatest God dream** or we can choose to stay still and possibly miss out on a gift He wanted to give.

Take this little mantra that I learnt years ago at a conference to remind you on days when it feels hard.

*"If I always do what I have always done,
I will always get what I have always gotten."*

Be - committed to
Do - what it takes to
Have - what you want

I am excited for you as you take these essential and significant steps towards walking more fully in your greatness and into the woman that God designed and created you to be.

SELF-CARE

Invite a trusted friend to go for a coffee, share your dreams and goals with each other. Take time to laugh and enjoy friendship. Part of self-care is taking care of your relationships and part of conquering your goals is sharing them with a trusted friend. This sharing makes the dream and goal become more of a reality.

HOMEWORK

Review your goals every day for the next month. Read it, say it. Ex--ample: "When I am a teacher", "When I go to Greece".

Make your goals as your opening screen on your phone and/or computer as a reminder of your goal. Of why you get up early each morning and persevere when you feel like giving up.

In the next segment we will explore your purpose and why. This adds a whole new dynamic to staying in the 'go zone' for goals.

MY PRAYER FOR YOU TODAY

"Papa, you say that 'You know the plans You have for Your beautiful daughter (your name). Open her heart, mind and eyes to dream big dreams with You in the next days, weeks and months. Let her hear Your voice and the peace that comes when she walks in alignment with You and Your plans for her. Give her a newfound passion and confidence to set goals and make plans knowing that You will guide her even when she feels fearful of the walk before her. Give her a passion and joy and sense of fulfillment as she leans into the dreams You have planted in her heart. Amen."

CHAPTER SEVEN
LIFE COMPASS

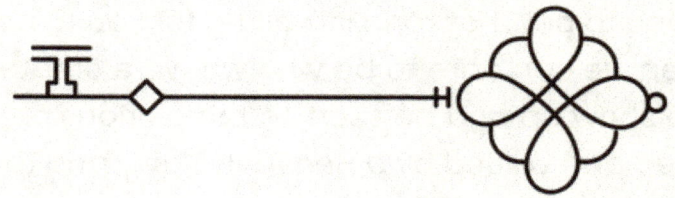

GROUNDING EXERCISE

Find a space to relax and get comfortable - put some soaking worship music on to help you relax.

- Pause
- Close your eyes
- Picture a peaceful place, either in real life or an imaginary place in your mind.
- Invite Jesus into the picture... Where is He? *(holding you, dancing with you, carrying you or walking to meet you?)*
- Take five deep breaths *(with each inhale, breath in the peace, with each exhale, picture the stresses of the day leaving your body)*
- Focus on your 4 senses, one at a time
    - What do I feel?
    - What do you see?
    - What do I smell?
    - What do I hear?

Notice how you feel after you have completed this grounding exercise. Notice the muscle tension, has it been released? This breathing exercise is meant to ground you in preparation for today's module.

SONG OF THE DAY

Is there a song your heart is singing today? **Reflect on the song suggestions below by Stars Go Dim and Tenille**

1. [Stars Go Dim - You Are Loved](#)
2. [Tenille - Dare to Be](#)

I dare you to be! The world is waiting for you to be you. It is one of the precious moments in life when we can dare to be who we were created and designed to be by our Creator... to dare to show up and be seen as the glorious creature He made you as. To know that you are loved and valued by a Heavenly Papa and to let that shine.

PRAYER

"Papa, walk with me through this module, teach me to see as You see. Help me to value what You value. Let Your values be what guides my every thought and action.
Papa, show me today how you see me. Let me know Your love for me in a new way. Show me what is important to you and the unique way that you have made me, so I can stand on Your love and live my life out of that place of love. Amen"

LET'S BEGIN

You have done some really difficult and soul-searching work. **You can be incredibly proud of yourself**. Do a check in with yourself and tune in to how you are feeling with the work you have done. You might be feeling lighter, exhausted, worn thin, hopeful, courageous. There is no wrong feeling, just tune in and sense where you are at.

In this segment you are going to look at what is important to you in life. **I call these foundational values - Your life compass.**

What are **foundational** values and why are they important?

I like how John C Maxwell states it:

"Your core values are the deeply held beliefs that authentically describe your soul."

Your foundational values are a personal code for guiding your choices, actions, behaviors and responses. They are what guides your decisions in your personal life, relationships, business, career, your family life and your choices and behaviors. They are your life compass.

Discovering your personal foundational values will provide you with greater understanding and awareness of who you are, why you make the decisions you make, and do the things you do, helping you maximize your potential as a person.

I also like to look at **foundational values as a compass in life that guides us. A compass that God gave us when He create**d each of us. When you do not operate in your values and honor them, you will have a difficulty in achieving your fullest God-given potential. Life is automatically in more of an alignment and flow when we let our core values be a compass.

> *"Peace of mind comes when your life is in harmony with true principles and values and in no other way."* - Stephen Covey

It can also be easy to live by values someone else has put on us if we are not in tune to our values and daily checking in on our personal values compass.

Most of us don't know **or understand** our values. We don't understand what's most important to us. rather, we put our focus and beliefs on what our society, culture, **family of origin and media tells us.**

Living life without a sense or understanding of our foundational values is like walking into a store and buying a pair of jeans with our eyes closed. We are there but not seeing what we are purchasing, likely we will purchase something that does not fit and makes us feel uncomfortable and dissatisfied. So, it is with our values. Living outside of our **foundational** values can leave us feeling frustrated and discontent with our lives and circumstances that happen.

Every situation in life is controlled by your beliefs and **by your** values.

Values are a strong foundation from which we base our thinking, choices, behaviors, actions and even, conversations from. They tell a story about who we are, what we believe in and why we are the way we are. They tell a story of the **unique character and nature of you.**

When you have a solid sense of yourself and live from your **foundational** value, **you are living from the essence of who God created you to be. Your unique beautiful self.**

When we honor our personal **foundational** values on a consistent basis, we experience fulfillment, happiness and **a sense of purpose and meaning in life and an alignment with God.**

What you value is where you place your time and attention, it is what you focus on. Are you focusing on what is most important to you?

When you align with your values, and what you desire in life, you will experience a sense of fulfillment and accomplish your goals with a greater sense of ease, alternatively, when your values are not in alignment with your vision and purpose for your life there will be an unrest and an enormous amount of grit, push and effort. By acknowledging and taking responsibility for the life that you have created, you are taking the first step to aligning your values. You will look at what is MOST important to you and choose beliefs and values according to your vision.

Your values will **be a light on the path** to your vision. Your compass. **They will light up in your heart** knowing that you are on the right path. They will help you to evaluate decisions and choices that are before you. Your values will inspire you to make decisions that create a sense of empowerment within you. **They are your 'decision making blueprint'.**

God created you with a specific set of **foundational** values, as you have lived life, your experiences have also shaped and influenced your values. Above everything else, is a voice that holds the compass, I like this verse from Jeremiah 30:21 NIV:

"Whether you turn to the right or to the left, your ears will hear a voice behind you, saying, "This is the way; walk in it."

Knowing your **foundational** values will help you to set boundaries and to say 'yes' to the things that are in alignment with those values and to say 'no' to the things that are not aligning. Stephen Covey expresses it this way:

"Begin each day with the blueprint of my deepest values FIRMLY in mind then when challenges come, make decisions BASED on those values."

Your *personal* values are an **essential part of who you are, and who you want to be.** Exploring and discovering your **foundational** values is a challenging, insightful and important exercise.

DIGGING DEEPER – Reflect and Journal

Identify a time that you were the happiest in your life.

Identify a time that was most meaningful to you.

What was meaningful about this occasion?

What were you doing?

What values were you honoring?

Identify a time when you felt the proudest?

What were you doing?

What factors contributed to the proud moment?

What values were you honoring in this moment?

Consider times that you felt the most fulfilled and content.

What factors contributed to the feelings of fulfillment and contentment?

How did this experience give your life meaning?

What values were you honoring in this experience?

Now let's explore the opposite: identify a time that you felt angry, upset or frustrated. What was happening for you in this moment?

What values were being suppressed **or opposed** at this moment?

VALUES DISCOVERY

What are your **personal** foundational values? Spend some time in reflection - **What insight did you gain from the questions above?** What is most important to you? What you cannot live without in your life; spiritually physical emotional, relational, What makes you feel like you are aligned and happy - you and what you are doing is right with the world in this moment?

A quick Internet search for 'core or personal values' may lead you to tools to assist you in refining this discovery of your foundational values.

Journal your insights and reflections on this page. Define your foundational values - the bottom line of what you cannot live without in your life. The essence of you!
Example: compassion, drive, fun, harmony

List your top **6 can't live without foundational** values below in order of importance to alignment in your life. What **6 foundational values are my life compass and essential to my life?**

1. _____

2. _____

3. _____

4. _____

5. _____

6. _____

REFLECTION

Let's take a closer look at these **6 foundational** values. Do your values align with God's word for your life?

Do you feel your values are in the order of importance to you?
(*list them in order of importance*)

1. _____

2. _____

3. _____

4. _____

5. _____

6. _____

Which values are essential to supporting 'who you are'?

Which values represent your behaviors and actions - your primary way of being?

Are these values personal to you? Explain

Do these values resonate and give you a sense of peace and belonging?

Do these values feel consistent with who you are or do they represent a value that was placed on you by someone else? Example. A parent, society, authority figure

What's your level of satisfaction of how each value is honored in your life? Score each of your top **6 foundational** values below.

| Not Honoured | Somewhat Honoured | Fully Honoured |

0_____ 5 _____ 10

This exercise brings awareness to how each value is expressed in your day-to-day life. If you scored below a 7, ask yourself what changes do you need to make in order to more fully honor this particular value?

When was a time you fully embraced your most important values?

How have you honored your values and how did you feel?

What are some ways you can lean more fully into your values?

Did you risk, in honor of holding true to your values? What are your risking.

"As you live your values, your sense of identity, integrity, control, and inner-directedness will infuse you with both exhilaration and peace. You will define yourself from within, rather than by people's opinions or by comparisons to others." - Stephen Covey

Do a check-in with your personal **foundational** values again:

Do you feel a difference in your level of fulfillment and contentment in life as you **imagine** living in your foundational values and begin to **live** in your foundational values?

At this moment, how would you fill in the following blank using one word:

"At my core I am _____". *(List value)*

As you learn to lean into your values, you will begin to let the values define your decision making and the direction the compass points, for all your life choices. As opportunities are presented you can ask yourself, "Does this opportunity align with what I believe in?"

Most important is this next question, **"Does this value align with what God wants for my life and with who He says I am?"**

When you feel a restlessness, unease or discontent, ask yourself 'which value am I not honoring in this moment? How am I not aligning with what Jesus wants for me?

Let your foundational values be a compass for your life. Make it a habit to check-in daily with your life compass. Your values will impact your career, relationship, family, and personal decisions.

By staying in tune to your values you will be tapping in daily to the **greatness that lies within you and who God says you are.**

Let His word guide you and continue to show you the **values He has placed in you.**

"Trust in the LORD with all your heart, and do not lean on your own understanding. In all your ways acknowledge him, and he will make straight your paths." - Proverbs 3:5-6

SELF-CARE

Schedule self-care time in your calendar like you would schedule in an important appointment. Plan time for some fun. Schedule 2 – 3 selfcare activities in your calendar this week.

HOMEWORK

Write your values on a paper, sticky note or your phone's home screen. Somewhere that you can see it every day. Take 5 minutes each day to read them and reflect on how you are honoring your values that day.

MY PRAYER FOR YOU TODAY

"Papa, as this beautiful woman has dug deeper in this module and come to an even greater understanding of what You have placed inside her, I pray her confidence in who she is will continue to also grow and become deeply rooted in You. I pray that her heart will continue to walk in the values that lie waiting to be honored. Give her courage to walk in the way that You have set before her. Let her feel Your divine love for her today! Amen."

CHAPTER EIGHT

YOU SHINE

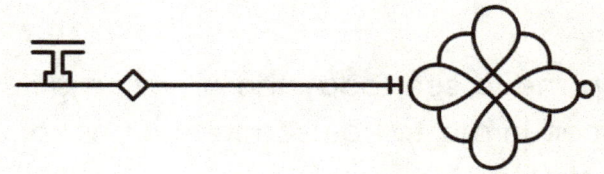

GROUNDING EXERCISE

Find a space to relax and get comfortable - put some soaking **music on as you quiet your mind and prepare your heart for todays chapter has for you.**

- Pause
- Close your eyes
- Picture a peaceful place, either in real life or an imaginary place in your mind.
- Invite Jesus into the picture… Where is He? *(holding you, dancing with you, carrying you or walking to meet you?)*
- Take five deep breaths *(with each inhale, breath in the peace, with each exhale, picture the stresses of the day leaving your body)*
- Focus on your 4 senses, one at a time
    - What do I feel?
    - What do you see?
    - What do I smell?
    - What do I hear?

Notice how you feel after you have completed this grounding exercise. Notice the muscle tension, has it been released? This breathing exercise is meant to ground you in preparation for today's module.

SONG OF THE DAY

Prepare your heart for more by listening to music. Below is **suggested music by John Denver and Travis Green / Steffany Gretzinger that has be**en chosen for you. Be still and let the music and words speak to you.

1. [John Denver - The Gift You Are](#)
2. [Good And Loved - Travis Greene (feat. Steffany Gretzinger) Lyric Video](#)

PRAYER

"God help me to see today the amazing gifts you have given me and the strengths you have placed in me, to be used for your honor and glory. Open my heart and eyes to more of You in my life."

LET'S BEGIN

If someone asked you today what are your gifts and strengths? How would you respond? And how quickly can you respond if you are asked what your flaws and weaknesses are? We are often quick to focus on our weaknesses and are unsure about our gifting and strengths.

In this segment we are going to explore what your gifts and strengths are and how knowing your strengths, that are a part of your unique personality style can greatly benefit your life.

One of the most powerful tools in life is to know your strengths and accept the incredible gift they are to you and **the incredible gift YOU are to the world around you**. God made you with special and unique strengths and when you hide your strengths and do not use them, you are missing out, and so are others. **You are designed and created uniquely with a unique set of strengths** for a reason and when you do not show up with those strengths...the world misses out.

This verse in Psalms written by King David expresses how He thinks of you:

"I praise you, for I am fearfully and wonderfully made. Wonderful are your works; my soul knows it very well." - Psalm 139:14

You are fearfully and wonderfully made, all your idiosyncrasies, your strengths and even those weaknesses that you get ashamed of. He made you with a specific set of strengths and **He did not make a mistake when He made you**, remember, you are fearfully and wonderfully made.

WHAT IS A GIFT OR STRENGTH?

Strengths are personal abilities that come naturally to you. Abilities that you excel at. I like to call these gifts. **A gift is something you are born with and comes naturally to you.**

Those who use their natural strengths and gifts achieve the most in life as they are operating out of a natural flow

So, it is important to be self - aware. Knowing yourself, what your strengths and weaknesses are can help you know where you need to focus on improvement and where you can focus for greater results.

We do not usually enjoy looking at our flaws, but so often tend to do so, letting the inner judge highlight when we are not at our best. It is important to take an objective look at yourself to identify what your strengths and weaknesses are so you can **more fully walk in your strengths and take a constructive approach to your weaknesses.** When you can identify your weaknesses, you can learn to consciously develop these areas or outsource them where possible.

You might ask... What Is the difference between a strength and a value? Strengths are a part of the character that is a natural part of a person which, when you are using your strengths, it brings a sense of authenticity, and a feeling of excitement while displaying them.

A value is like a life compass, bringing direction into your one amazing life.

Why is it so important to know your best **gifts and s**trengths?

Individuals that know their strengths are more confident, self-accepting and have a higher self-esteem. They tend to be happier and more satisfied with life, experiencing less stress and knowing how to utilize their strengths to assist them through stressful situations. Knowing your strengths will instill feelings of authenticity and a more positive mindset. **When you know the gifts and strengths, God has given you, your choices and behaviors will be more in tune with what you do best and excel in.**

Focusing on what you do well, and the strengths God gave you, instead of on your flaws will have a real positive impact on your lifestyle and sense of well-being by fully developing and applying your strengths. When you function in your **gifts and strengths** you will feel natural at using your abilities and further developing them.

A sense of positive energy and aligning with God comes along with using **gifts and** strengths and will flow together with your **foundational** values, satisfying an inner need to live in a place of using your best gifts and to continue applying them to your daily life.

Knowing and focusing on your gifts and strengths will extend the vision you have of yourself, who God made you to be and what you are capable of doing with this life you are given.

Some of your **gifts and** strengths you will recognize in yourself already, while others will be more subtle and difficult to identify.

MINING FOR GOLD

You are uniquely you, designed and created by a Heavenly Creator with a special set of strengths, traits and gifts. We often do not recognize these qualities in ourselves until we dig for them, examining and looking at our behaviors and actions, acknowledging where we excel.

Answer the following questions to mine for the strengths that you may not have seen in yourself. **Take some time to list your talents, skills, characteristics, behaviors, and areas of greatest knowledge.** It may feel difficult and like self-bragging but give yourself permission to acknowledge where you shine.

What activities were you naturally drawn to as a child?

What is easy and effortless for you to do today? What comes naturally?

What do you do especially well?

What is enjoyable and fun for you to do?

What are your greatest successes? Why?

What are your strongest character traits?

What energizes you?

What activity gives you a sense of fulfillment and purpose?

What makes you unique?

What activities or tasks do you gravitate to and do effortlessly?

When you have time to do something you truly enjoy, what are you doing?

When you find yourself in the "zone or flow" what are you doing?

What activities do you get completely absorbed in?

What qualities do you have that you could not do life without?

What is the most enjoyable job/career you have had?

What was it about this job/career that you enjoyed the most?

What would your closest friend say are your **gifts** / qualities/strengths?

List gifts and strengths you use to help others and create joy for another?

When do you feel most in alignment with God and His call on your life?

WHAT ARE YOUR GIFTS AND STRENGTHS?

Brain dump - Create an exhaustive list of the gifts and strengths that God has placed inside you - from the questions above and what you instinctively know are a part of who you are.

List your top 5 gifts and strengths.

1. _____
2. _____
3. _____
4. _____
5. _____

Which **gifts and** strengths are most important with accomplishing your **life goals**? *(refer back to module 6)*

Which **gifts and** strengths will best help you to become the person you want to be? The person God created you to be?

Reflect on compliments you have been given! What do others see in you that create the compliment?

Do these compliments align with your **gifts and** strengths? If so, how?

JOURNAL

Be still and ask Papa what He wants to show you about the **gifts and** strengths He put in you and if there are any strengths that you have missed.

IDENTIFYING WEAKNESSES

Now that you have listed your strengths, let's take a brief moment to examine weaknesses that you have. Everyone has weaknesses and it is important to know both, what your strengths and your weaknesses are, so that you can **learn to manage them**.

When you know your weaknesses, **you can say 'yes' to the things that energize you and bring a sense of purpose to your life and 'no' to the activities that don't serve your greater purpose and life goals** or learn how to 'staff' your weaknesses.

What are the weaknesses that you are aware of?

What do you tend to avoid?

What causes you to 'give up' when tackling a project?

What is an energy drainer for you?

What would you call your blind-spot? (An area you struggle to understand or see the importance of)

What holds you back from moving forward? What is your roadblock?

While awareness of weaknesses is good, it is important for you to keep your focus on your strengths **as 'what you focus on' is the direction you go**. **Be aware** of what your blind spots are and **focus on the strengths and giftings you have.**

JOURNAL

Ask Papa what He would like to show you about the weaknesses you have identified. Does He have a different and new perspective for you?

STRENGTHS

As you step more fully into your 'you', you will choose which behaviors and activities you wish to eliminate, strengthen or change in **order to walk more fully in your unique and deeper purpose, aligning more fully with God's design for you.**

A strength will give you energy when you are actively using it, you will feel motivated with a sense of enjoyment and fulfillment. It will feel more natural to you and a part of who you are.

There may be strengths that you have that have been suppressed in life and may need some coaxing to flourish. It doesn't mean this is not a strength, it just may take some **'stepping out of your comfort zone'.**

Your **gifts and** strengths are what come naturally to you, when you discover your greatest strengths, you learn to use them to handle stress and challenges, you can improve your life and thrive in all areas as you become happier, and develop healthy relationships with those who matter most to you.

I highly value how Gallup describes strengths:

> *"Excellence, not average, is your measure. Taking something from below average to slightly above average takes a great deal of effort and in your opinion is not very rewarding. Transforming something strong into something superb takes just as much effort but is much more thrilling. Strengths, whether yours or someone else's, fascinate you. Like a diver after pearls, you search them out, watching for the telltale signs of a strength. A glimpse of untutored excellence, rapid learning, a skill mastered without recourse to steps — all these are clues that a strength may be in play. And having found a strength, you feel compelled to nurture it, refine it, and stretch it toward excellence. You polish the pearl until it shines. This natural sorting of strengths means that others see you as discriminating. You choose to spend time with people who appreciate your particular strengths. Likewise, you are attracted to others who seem to have found and cultivated their own strengths. You tend to avoid those who want to fix you and make you well rounded. You don't want to spend your life bemoaning what you lack. Rather, you want to capitalize on the gifts with which you are blessed. It's more fun. It's more productive. And, counterintuitively, it is more demanding."* (www.gallup.com/cliftonstrengths).

You will strengthen your strength muscles by using them.

Be adventurous and step outside your comfort zone, <u>often</u>. Growth happens outside the comfort zone and your **gifts and** strengths will shine when you use them.

Another quick Internet search for strengths may lead you to tools to assist you in refining this discovery of your gifts and strengths.

JOURNAL

Reflect on the insights have you gained from this module and the exercises? Journal the insights you have gained. Were you surprised by the gifts and strengths that you discovered? Did you gain a greater clarity for why you do some of the things you do? Maybe a deeper understanding of His divine purpose over your life?

SELF-CARE

Step outside your comfort zone today. Find one activity that stretches you, yes this is part of self-care. Put on your favorite music and dance for 5 minutes or more. Dance with your partner, your friends, your children or dance solo. Just dance. Feel the energy!

HOMEWORK

Ask ten people who know you well to write down the strengths and gifts they see in you when they have witnessed you at your best. You may ask "how do you experience me?. Ask individuals that come from diverse backgrounds including friends, mentors, family, colleagues, managers, etc.

Identify patterns among the feedback you receive. Which strengths do you see repeated? Create a word self-portrait, outlining the strengths you discovered in yourself, and the strengths as perceived by the sources above who know you and have seen you at your best. Put your strengths to work and shine!

MY PRAYER FOR YOU TODAY

"Papa, I thank you for the beautiful strengths you have put in this amazing woman. I pray she has a deeper understanding and knowing of the love You have for her. That her feelings of unworthiness and unlovable are replaced with a deep fulfilling sense of Your love and presence. I pray that she can accept her weaknesses and embrace her strengths using them to honor and glorify You. Give her a deeper understanding of where You want her to use these strengths and how to continue growing them and to use them with boldness. Take all shame and guilt off of her and let her feel a sense of freedom to boldly step into Your fullness for her. Amen."

CHAPTER NINE
MINING DEEPER FOR GOLD

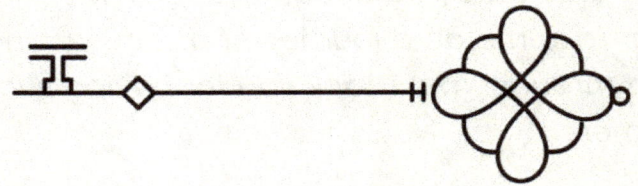

GROUNDING EXERCISE

Find a space to relax and get comfortable - put some soaking music on to prepare your heart for today's chapter as you explore your purpose and why.

- Pause
- Close your eyes
- Picture a peaceful place, either in real life or an imaginary place in your mind.
- Invite Jesus into the picture... Where is He? *(holding you, dancing with you, carrying you or walking to meet you?)*
- Take five deep breaths *(with each inhale, breath in the peace, with each exhale, picture the stresses of the day leaving your body)*
- Focus on your 4 senses, one at a time
    - What do I feel?
    - What do you see?
    - What do I smell?
    - What do I hear?

Notice how you feel after you have completed this grounding exercise. Notice the muscle tension, has it been released? This breathing exercise is meant to ground you in preparation for today's module.

SONG OF THE DAY

Prepare your heart for more by listening to music. Below is a song suggestion by Fearless Soul and Bethseda   usic that has been chosen for you. Be still and let the words of the music speak to your heart as you listen.

- [This Song Will Remind You to Love WHO YOU ARE (Meant For You)Fearless Soul](#)
- [Wide Eyed Wonder - Bethseda Music](#)

PRAYER

"Papa, I pray today that you will open my heart and ears to hear your desires and purpose for me. Take me on a journey of discovery and let each thought and idea that comes be filtered through You. Thank you for having such a unique and intricate plan for me. Guide me! Amen."

LET'S BEGIN

How does one define 'life purpose"?

There comes a **defining moment** in life, when you feel that what you're doing **aligns with God's plan for your life**, your head and your heart, and with the giftings, strengths, values and talents you have, while you are making a difference and filling a need in the world around you.

I like this quote by John Maxwell:

"Your calling is your purpose with a divine touch."

When you have a sense of your life purpose and know your 'WHY' - you are doing what you love to do. You no longer just go through the motions but **rather become intentional with your day to day actions and decisions.**

There comes a time in most of our lives, where we ask a far-reaching question. 'What am I on this earth for?" 'What purpose does God want me to fulfill?"

We may spend months and years searching for the answer to this question and feel frustrated if we do not know 'now' what purpose we have.

You may feel that there is no purpose for your life, but look closely at the following verses:

"For I know the plans I have for you," declares the LORD, "plans to prosper you and not to harm you, plans to give you hope and a future." - Jeremiah 29:11

"Before I formed you in the womb I knew you, and before you were born, I consecrated you; I appointed you a prophet to the nations". - Jeremiah 1:5

As you can see from the verses above, **God has a plan for you.** His purpose for your life so often goes so far beyond what you can imagine that it may scare you into a paralyzing fear if you knew the extent of what He desires for you, and for each of His daughters.

Spend intentional time with Jesus and ask Him what He dreams for you. Dream big with Him for your future and life purpose.

Your life purpose becomes a **motivating influence** - while it guides your life decisions, actions and behaviors, it also helps to shape your goals and gives you a sense of direction. It creates a desire for every day to be more meaningful and to have a **greater impact on the world around you**, filling a void in your life and a void or need in the world.

You may even wonder if you have a purpose and feel like you don't have a place on this earth. I am here to tell you; **you do have a purpose and a reason for being.** You are valued and desperately needed, someone somewhere needs You, they need you and your story to encourage them to keep going. They need you to be the difference for them. You have a purpose, and the exciting part is, if you are unsure what it is, **you get to go on a journey with Jesus to discover what that is for you.**

Within each of us there lies an innate desire to make a difference. As a young child and teen years, especially as we neared the end of high school years, there was always a question that carried a certain mystery in it. 'What do you want to be when you grow up?' as we become adults that question often still has an evasive ring to it. Who do I want to be? How can I make a difference or an impact?

Oft times, this is overwhelming to understand and figure out and we wish someone would just stand behind us, put a hand on our shoulder and another pointing the way ahead saying this is the way to go, this is how you make a difference, go and do it, this is your purpose"

It's not quite that easy...figuring out your life purpose is something only you can explore and find the answer to.

The answer lies within you, it is like mining for gold, the deeper you dig into discovering more about yourself the more you will discover the passions that are waiting to be exposed.

It is often a process of life experiences that slowly brings to light the purpose burning in our hearts. Life experiences, the good, the bad and the ugly, peel back the layers and prepare us for that greater purpose. It is like the refining fire, or the potter and the clay, molding us through life experiences until the shaping has created **God-centered desires within us**.

While you are being shaped and molded, **be intentional to be the best version of who God created and designed you to be.** When you live with gratitude and intention you are living a life on purpose. To lead a life on purpose, follow the passions of your heart, the ones that Jesus places there. Follow what makes your heart sing and feel full! There is not just one purpose for you, there may be multiple passions that you have that all make up your uniquely designed purpose and meaning for life.

I am a mom. That is a life purpose for me. To be the best mom I can be and to raise my young men into men of honor. I also have another passion I call a purpose and that is helping you to see the beauty and uniqueness that makes you the **spectacular and amazing woman that you are**. Another purpose of mine is to make a difference in the lives of women across the globe, inspiring and motivating you to be the best version of you, to tell you about God's great love and design for you and your life.

Purpose in life is to love life fully by putting ourselves completely into showing up and stepping boldly into what you are passionate about and what excites you. This will mean grabbing a hold of God's promises, keeping your eyes fixed firmly on Him while stepping into the unknown with shaky legs and doing what is before you, regardless of how inadequate you feel for the job at hand. **It is showing up and letting yourself be seen where God is calling you to be seen.**

The feeling that something is missing in your life can be a gift as it is inviting you to explore and discover what brings you a sense of fulfillment and passion. When you don't feel connected in life, **it is an opportunity for self-discovery and digging deeper into more of an awareness of what God desires for you and what really matters to you and your heart desires. It is an invitation to spend more time with Him and hear His heart for you.**

Darlene Brock expresses it this way –

> *"Within us is everything we need, to become who we are to become,*
> *it just needs to be mined and nurtured and developed,*
> *it takes grit to discover it and grace to fail in the process."*

Oftentimes, we look at our life story and wonder what good can come from it, however, our greatest purpose in life may come directly from the messiness of the story. When you can take your mess and turn it into a message that impacts someone's life you may be offering the greatest hope, encouragement and inspiration to change a life.

Your mess may be the catalyst for someone else's victory and healing!

Messes, accomplishments, and goals, big and small, can be the stepping-stones to a fulfilled, passionate life that you get to create.

By uncovering your gifts, talents and passions **you can light the world up by showing up and being the best version of who God created you to be.**

God is going to prompt and guide your heart, and this is going to be the guidepost for accessing your passions and purposes in life. When you are inspired, connected and feel like your heart is full you will be motivated to explore and to gain valuable insight into what brings you the most joy and happiness.

MINING DEEPER FOR GOLD

Let's begin exploring some aspects of your life that you may deem as unimportant but are insightful to your life purpose. Connect the dots from your childhood, through your teen years and into adulthood. How have you always made a positive difference in people's lives?

What did you love to do as a child? What did you excel at? What made you feel proud, accomplished and happy?

What makes you feel that way now?

Describe a time in your life - a specific experience - where you felt you were fully alive, as if were doing what you were born to do?

What do you excel at in life as an adult?

What matters most in life to you?

What solution would you like to bring to the world?

What makes your heart expand and feel determined?

What would you do if you knew you couldn't fail?

What would you do even if nobody paid you to do it?

What makes you come alive?

What activities would bring you more joy and meaning?

What makes you cry, or makes you angry?

If it were not for money, time, and personal responsibilities what would you really love to do with your life?

If you were free to do whatever you wanted, you had nothing stopping you such as time or money, what would you begin doing tomorrow morning?

Do you see a pattern emerging from your answers to the questions? Do you feel a tug at your heartstrings in a specific direction? Explain.

What do you feel or sense God prompting you to do? Does this align with the above questions?

Your actions help to define the purpose you have in life. **Intentionally taking action is an essential step towards becoming more grounded in who you are meant to be and do.** At the end of life, what do you want to be remembered for?

If you were to write an obituary for yourself, what would you want it to say? What legacy do you want to leave behind? How will the world be a better place because you lived?

Write a paragraph, as if you were writing your obituary, what do you want to be remembered for?

Picture yourself again at your 90th birthday party? Who is there with you celebrating this amazing life you have lived? What accomplishments are you celebrated for? What milestones are remembered and celebrated? Create a picture in your mind's eye of you. Did you fulfill your goals? Did you take action and live a fulfilled life, one full of action? Are you someone that lived life to the fullest, no questions asked, who relentlessly pursued every opportunity that came your way with confidence, and a zest and zeal for life? Can you say you lived without regrets of having pursued your hearts desires and made a lasting impact on the people around you?

Journal the above picture - Your 90th birthday celebration.

YOUR PURPOSE

The key to uncovering your life purpose **is to spend intimate time with the greatest Counselor and Coach of all, your Heavenly Father, asking Him to speak into your life and to guide you,** then begin living as if you have already reached the goal and are living out of a place of purpose.

It takes dedication, perseverance and hard work to achieve **the fulfilling life of living in your God-designed purpose.** It does not happen overnight. **Honoring what you love to do** and moving away from what exhausts and drains you. It takes stepping outside of your comfort zone over and over again.

It takes making changes and taking charge of your life. Remember the feeling of being at your 90th birthday party and celebrating You and all your accomplishments over the last 9 decades. Let that feeling fuel your drive to keep going even when it is hard, to keep **discovering the greatness of who you are and what you were placed on this earth for.**

When you allow the positive qualities within you that bring you a sense of meaning, delight and purpose will be amplified and allowed to shine more brightly creating a **God-confidence overflow** to those you come in contact with.

Together with God, YOU are your life on purpose!

Knowing your life purpose and what fulfills you may compel you to take on challenges that will stretch you as much as they inspire you. When you're motivated and empowered by a clear purpose and know that you are in alignment with God, there is very little that will hold you back from **accomplishing what lights your heart and soul up.**

BOOK TITLE

If you were to write a book of your life story until today. What would the title of your book be?

Spend some time on this question, put some thought into it as it can have a profound effect on how you view your story and the impact it has today.

If you were to write a book of your life story until today. What would the title of your book be?

DEFINING YOUR WHY

Your WHY is the one constant that will guide you toward fulfillment in your work and life. It is the purpose, cause or belief that drives every one of us.

Knowing what your 'why' is will help you to stay committed to your dreams and goals and will keep you focused on action steps needed to reach a place of fulfillment. It is the reason that drives you to do what you do, the real deepest reason for striving to reach your life purpose.

When you are in a place of discouragement and wondering what is next, your 'why' will be the light that guides you.

Your why is tied to your passions and your purpose, and is reflected in what excites you, what makes you happy, how you can serve the world, and what your strengths and talents are as we explored previously.

REFLECTION

- What makes you excited?
- What energizes you to jump out of bed in the morning?
- What am I naturally good at?
- What do other people ask me to do?
- What makes you happy?
- If money were no object, what would you do?
- What causes a positive ripple effect around me?

Brain Dump

Write fast and steady. Write your answers to the above questions and anything else that comes to mind, write non-stop, anything that comes to your mind, this is not a thinking exercise but rather another brain dump.

Do you see a pattern that emerged in the brain dump?

Fill in the following statement - insert your goal and your reason for the goal.

I want to _____

so that _____.

Dig deep here and continue asking WHY? This is important... as you mine down into what really matters to you it will become clearer to you what your why is.

Continue making statements, asking why? after each statement you create until there is no further answer. Keep in mind a God perspective, is there a God 'why'?

> *Example:*
> *I want to make more money so that I can have freedom. Why?*
> *I want freedom so that I can travel and help people. Why?*
> *I want to travel and help people so that they can know Jesus. Why?*
> *I want people to know Jesus so that _____. Why?*

You get the idea... keep mining down until you have no further answers.

As you look at your final sentence, does it feel like a defining statement for you? Does it feel like your why?

Write your purpose and why statement. A why statement will be simple, clear, contributing, actionable and expressed in a language that affirms your purpose.

I want to _____

so that _____.

My WHY is – *"To empower and equip individuals in overcoming obstacles, discovering their God' beauty and who they are, so they can reach their goals and dreams while living uninhibited with boldness."* - Ellen Reimer

Write your purpose and why statement below:

Once you find the "Why "that speaks to your soul, your next question is, "What am I waiting for?" Ask yourself "what decision can I make right now that will spur me into action and help me to stay committed to living my purpose and why?"

When you know your 'why' and live out of a place of 'purpose', you let your **inner light shine to the world around you.** The most beautiful space is when **you know how deeply loved you are by your Heavenly Papa and how beautiful He has made you**, from that place you can live your purpose with a bold authenticity, letting your true self shine, your God-confidence.

SELF-CARE

Alone Time. This is easy for some people and very difficult for others. Being comfortable in your own presence is so important. **Create space to spend alone time with Jesus, ask Him about the dreams He has for you, take time to listen and to just simply enjoy being with Him.** Create some space for alone time this week. It may be going to the movies solo, sitting in a coffee shop or an evening at home alone to do what you want. Reflect on the hard work you have done, be proud of you.

Do something that made you happy as a child. Do it unashamedly. When was the last time you felt carefree and deliriously happy? Go do something that makes you feel carefree and giddy with happiness and fun.

HOMEWORK

Write your Why Statement somewhere that you will see it every day. When you feel that you have come up against a wall or feel like giving up, read your Why Statement until you feel the courage to keep pushing forward. **Let your Why statement be a call to your soul each day to show up and shine.**

MY PRAYER FOR YOU TODAY

"Papa, I pray today that (your name) will feel her heart overflowing with love for You and with Your love for her. I pray that the passion that has been burning in her heart, even if it has just been a small flicker, can begin to burn ever so brightly as You prepare her for 'her reason', her purpose for being on this planet, whether it seems big or small to her, that she will know her greatness and the importance of Your purpose and hand over her life. O Papa, let her know the beauty that is within her, let her know that as she shows up as her true self, the glorious creature you made her to be, this is part of a purpose and that those she crosses paths with each day will feel touched by You, because you are so near her, and that their lives will be forever changed by experiencing the nearness of Your presence. May her light and purpose shine bright as a lighthouse beacon, offering hope and love to those that are near her. Bless her today and bless her life with your abundance and love. Amen"

CHAPTER TEN
BEAUTIFUL AUTHENTIC YOU

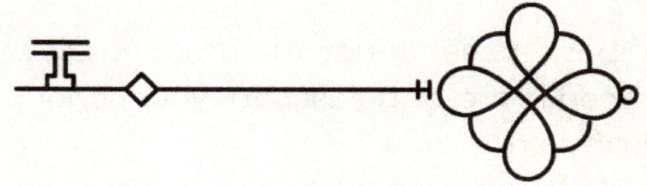

GROUNDING EXERCISE

Find a space to relax and get comfortable - put some worship soaking music on as you relax into this breathing exercise.

- Pause
- Close your eyes
- Picture a peaceful place, either in real life or an imaginary place in your mind.
- Invite Jesus into the picture… Where is He? *(holding you, dancing with you, carrying you or walking to meet you?)*
- Take five deep breaths *(with each inhale, breath in the peace, with each exhale, picture the stresses of the day leaving your body)*
- Focus on your 4 senses, one at a time
    - What do I feel?
    - What do you see?
    - What do I smell?
    - What do I hear?

Notice how you feel after you have completed this grounding exercise. Notice the muscle tension, has it been released? This breathing exercise is meant to ground you in preparation for today's module.

SONG OF THE DAY

Prepare your heart for more by listening to music. Below is a song suggestion that has been chosen for you. Be still and let the music and words speak to you. Listen to the words and let them soak in. icture esus reaching out is hand and inviting you into a beautiful dance with im. usic by ee Anne Womack

[Lee Anne Womack - I Hope You Dance](#)

PRAYER

"God help me to see today the amazing gifts you have given me and the strengths you have placed in me, to be used for your honor and glory. Open my heart and eyes to more of You in my life."

LET'S BEGIN

Wow. we have spent 9 weeks together. How are you doing? I wish I could sit down in a coffee shop with you and as we drink our lattes, I would love to hear how your experience has been the last 9 weeks. How is life different for you? Do you have a new perspective on your story and who you are as a woman? Do you feel God's love permeating your life? **Do you have a deeper understanding of His great love for you?**

Do you have **a renewed hope** for your future?

Do you have a deeper sense of knowing your value and worth?

"I wish you could see yourself today how other people see you, those that love you for who you are."

The **beautiful and courageous** woman that you are.

I wish you could see yourself how our Heavenly Papa sees you, how He delights in you.

Today we are going to wrap up our time together in this lesson plan. I want to give you some takeaways as you move forward in your life.

First and foremost, you are so loved deeply by a Heavenly Father. YOU are the King's daughter, never forget that.

The greatest act that you can do for yourself, is to spend time with Jesus. This will look different for everyone, but there are some fundamentals that make a difference to your time with God.

Let your bible and a highlighter be your best friend. A mentor once said to me, 'when you read, have a highlighter ready and look for words that have meaning that you want to highlight'... do this with your Bible. Spending time in the word and in conversation with Papa, **this is where you will learn how He sees and loves you.** Turn distractions off, put on worship music, **invite Jesus into the moment with you and just enjoy spending time with Him, like you would with your best friend.**

Ask Him how he sees you? Ask Him what He wants to say to you today? **Listen.** So often we do all the talking in prayer, **what if you just listen, picture yourself leaning into Him and listen to His heartbeat. What is He saying?**

SELF-CARE

This needs to be an essential part of your every day. Not just every now and then, but every day.

Some people have the notion that self-care is some extravagant, expensive and time-consuming task that leaves a hole in the wallet. But I dare to differ with you on that. Selfcare is taking care of you. **Selfcare is being comfortable in your own presence**. It is taking a walk, having an exercise routine. You have only one body and your body's a vessel to be treasured and looked after. We cannot just go and buy another body like we do a new car or a new pair of shoes when the old ones wear out.

Selfcare is eating healthy and nutritional meals with the odd splurge of ice cream and chocolate. Everybody craves 'that' snack at some time in their week. Shh. I will tell you mine but don't tell anyone else. Pure peanut butter, pure dark chocolate, melted together. And then I love to dip apple pieces into it. This was passed onto me by a health nutritionist and is a favorite go to when I am craving a healthier dessert.

Having time for friends and family is a part of self-care and keeping a balance between work and social life. Check in with yourself often to see how you are doing here. It is really easy to get so preoccupied with the demands of life that we forget that a selfcare need is connection with your tribe.

Schedule 'you time' into your calendar as if it is an appointment with your client, boss, or dentist. You are important to show up for you.

Do what you love and what makes your soul sing. Play, take time to be silly, laugh, create opportunities for a good ole' belly laugh with someone you love. Dance, stop and smell the beauty of a flower, **jump in puddle**, make a paper airplane, maybe your self-care is to buy yourself a bouquet of flowers, it doesn't need to be the most expensive bundle of roses, if you are on a budget maybe the $4 bundle of Gerber daisies or tulips is your bright spot in the day.

GRATITUDE

Take time to **delight in the beauty around you**. Practice gratefulness, keep a gratitude journal.

Look for the little things to be thankful for. Look for the moments of joy and delight. Let yourself delight in the simple pleasures.
- my eyes
- the sunshine
- a warm house to live in
- a cozy blanket
- a listening ear
- laughter
- chocolate covered strawberry
- freshly laundered clothes
- a picnic
- the smell of fresh cut grass
- a perfect slice of juicy watermelon

The list goes on and on

A heart of gratitude shifts the mindset and shifts a day.

COMPARISON

You, yes **fire comparison**. Comparison kills joy, friendships and kindness. Stop comparing yourself to others. This is part of selfcare. Rather have a curiosity for yourself and what your beautiful self has to offer the world. **God made you and He did not make a mistake**. There is no one like you and when we compare and try so hard to fit in, you are robbing the world around you of the beauty of YOU. Stop scrolling through social media and focus on what truly brings you joy.

FIND YOUR TRIBE

This takes time but focus on spending time with those that bring you happiness, with those that let you be you, accept you for who you are while gently encouraging you to be the best version of you.

Be around those that bring out the best in you and you can bring out the best in them. There is a saying 'iron sharpens iron'. Find your tribe that accepts you and also challenges you because they see the greatness in you. They say we are the most like the 5 people we spend the most time with. There is power in choosing your inner circle wisely as you will eventually rise to the level of those you spend the most time with. Choose positive, supportive people to be in your inner circle. **Choose friends that you encourage and influence each other to lean into God's best for you.**

GIVE BACK TO THE WORLD

You create happiness by making others happy. There is a true gift in giving. Think of how it feels to wrap a gift and give it to a friend. It is true that the giver receives as much as the receiver.

Also be willing to receive. Many people have a difficult time receiving, whether it is a physical gift, a compliment or an act of kindness. Give yourself permission to receive. It is a gift to you and the other person.

CREATE EXPERIENCES

Having pleasurable and memorable experiences with those you care about creates a deeper and more meaningful connection and enhances your sense of self-worth and joy.

Whether you are creating spur of the moment experiences or planning activities in advance. Create moments for creating enjoyable experiences and memories. It may be a mini vacation, a massage, camping or a day trip to the nearest hot spring, exploring activities that **give you a sense of delight**.

Be aware of what and who your energy drainers are. Sometimes we cannot avoid energy drains, but just the simple act of awareness allows you to plan for extra selfcare time to recharge and rejuvenate your body, soul and mind.

LEARN TO SAY 'NO' AND WHEN TO SAY 'YES'.

Boundaries and healthy communication are an integral part of selfcare. Creating healthy boundaries will help you find your own happiness without letting others dictate it for you. Before saying yes to requests, think about if it's something you really want to do or if it aligns with your values. If it doesn't, politely decline, this is a part of healthy communication and is important for every relationship you have.

BE AWARE when the ego mind is creeping in and taking up space in your mind and behaviors. When we let fear, control, and other negative emotions control our minds, ego takes over and causes a disconnect from self and from others. Ask yourself 'is this moving towards connection or away from it?"

SELF-AWARENESS

Selfcare is a self-awareness of what causes a disconnect with yourself and with those around you and giving yourself permission to let go of what is damaging connection. When you feel fear, negativity, jealousy, or even a gossip attitude creep in, take it to Jesus, there is no better place to take these feelings and emotions than to Jesus. **I like to picture, crawling into my Heavenly Fathers lap and finding a safe and comforting place, a place that I feel protected, but where I can also learn from my mistakes without any judgment.**

Have a curiosity and a compassion for yourself.

These two words kept in your daily vocabulary in your mind will be a lifeline to your happiness and relationships.

Find moments for just delighting in life and the beauty around you. Create moments for joy! **You are worth it!**

"Life is a dance, whatever you do, keep dancing."

What are your greatest self-care acts that you can schedule into your daily/weekly calendar?

LETTER TO FUTURE SELF

Picture yourself in 5 years from now. What advice would you like to give yourself in 5 years from now? What goals are you setting now for yourself in 5 years, envision your future and what you are doing, remind yourself of this time and the values and strengths you have. What does the future 'you' need to know in 5 years from now?

Example of a letter written to my older self:

April 24, 2027

Dear future self,

Wow it is hard to believe that 5 years have flown by so fast. I can hardly believe everything that has happened. Do you remember that time when you questioned who you are? A lot has happened, some of which you hoped for, and some which you didn't dare to dream about at the time. Our family is doing well. The kids are great. It hasn't all been easy but look at the life you have created. You are a confident woman comfortable in your own skin. But I want to remind you to take care of yourself and take time to push the pause button. You have accomplished so many of your goals, I remember how fragile you were when you started on your own. You were so worried all the time, about making a living, about being a good provider, and being a good mom. Remember the funny part is that things picked up when you stopped trying so hard to make it all work. When you focused on the contribution instead – on making things other people found genuinely helpful and useful – all of the other things you wanted flowed from that.

Look at you now, I knew you could achieve your goals and make the impact that you always felt was on your heart to make. You are making a profound difference, offering hope and joy to so many souls. I am so proud of you.

If I have any advice for you, it's this: Breath. Think ten times bigger. A hundred times bigger. Don't limit yourself. Worry less, way less, about mistakes you might make and about what people think or about "who am I to attempt such a thing?" Dare to make a difference. Dare to make a splash. Not for yourself or for your business, but for other people. The world could still use it, maybe now more than ever. Go on a vacation. I know you just got back from one a few months ago but plan your next one and remember how you used to always want to take your children with. Do it again. Plan a girl's trip. And future self, don't hold onto grudges, but also set healthy boundaries. Say what needs to be said and love with compassion and curiosity. Remember to dance. Those dance lessons you took. You are a great dancer, dance every day. It keeps you young and full of laughter. Keep dreaming.

More than anything, spend more time with Jesus, and dear future self, listen… It is in the listening that you learn to recognize His voice and hear Him better. It is in this place that you will find direction, wisdom, comfort, and joy. It is here that you will find the answers to all your questions. Here you will find rest.

More than anything, always be you. Let your authentic beautiful you shine. Don't hide who you are and the gifts you have. Be authentically you. Dare to be bold.

With love,

Your younger self,"

Write a letter to your future self. Choose a time, 5 years, 10 years or 20 years. Some people write a letter for 5 years and once they open it and read it in 5 years, they write another letter for their future self.

REFLECTION

What are your wins today? Ask this question each day as a check-in. It can be easy to forget the accomplishments you make, but the little one's matter as much as the larger ones.

If this is the second time you were to live this day, how would you live this day differently?

Who needs you to be on your 'A' game?

If I was super bold, what would life look like?

Is it more painful to keep your true self and all your hopes, dreams, goals and desires locked up inside you because you never unlocked them and let them be seen and got started OR more painful to let the world see the real you, pursue your dreams, experience the journey and possibly fail but know that you gave it everything you had?

The power of the mind is truly amazing. The more you believe in yourself and who you are as a beautiful inspiring woman, the more easily and naturally you will reach your goal and dreams and walk in your **full identity in Christ with God-confidence**.

This assignment is an important exercise designed to help you embrace the positive beliefs of who you are. Use this exercise to **push beyond your comfort zone** and push past the 'do not brag' belief. Today give yourself permission to say it out loud.

Write an exhaustive list of who you are and who God says you are. Include your strengths, talents, education, experiences, characteristics, accomplishments, support systems and anything else you can think of.

> *Example: I am courageous, I am brave, I am bold, I am pretty, I am strong, I am healthy, I am a great friend, I am supportive.*

Use complete 'I' statements and sentences. Write as much as you can think of. Notice your feelings and emotions as you write. Write until you cannot think of anything else to write.

Stop and take a break, come back to your writing and begin again.

Do this 3 times. This serves two purposes. First when you take a break and then come back to your writing, you will be able to go deeper and uncover things that are not right at the surface. Second, as you begin again you will read what you have already written and create a mindset, strengthening your belief in what you have already written.

Chapter 10 | Beautiful Authentic You

POWER STATEMENT
Fill in the following blanks to complete your power statement.

I am _____

Your why: _____

> *Example:* "I am a bold and confident woman, loved by God, empowering and equipping individuals to discover who they are in Christ, so they can reach their goals and dreams while living uninhibited with boldness".

Put this statement up somewhere that you can see it every day. Make it your homepage on your phone or computer. Put it on your bathroom mirror with mascara or a dry erase marker. Say it and believe! This is who you are at the core of your being. This is the essence of who you are.

WORDS OF AFFIRMATION
List 10 people that you trust and ask them to send you words describing how they see you. "How do you experience me? Take these words and review them when you feel like you need a self-talk or a kick in the butt. Finale.

Believe in yourself. You are valuable and worthy. The world needs you to be on your A game! The world needs you to let that light inside you shine bright. The light that you have hidden, continue to let it shine bright as you have begun to do in the last 9 weeks.

"You have this one wild and precious life to live"

Will you choose to show up and live this amazing life you have as your true authentic self or wearing a mask of pretense? What would it be like to embrace the essence of who you are? What if you dared to embrace your imperfections and quirks and rather looked at these imperfections as a unique gift?

Brene Brown says:

> *"To be authentic, we must cultivate the courage to be imperfect - and vulnerable. We have to believe that we are fundamentally worthy of love and acceptance, just as we are. I've learned that there is no better way to invite more grace, gratitude and joy into our lives than by mindfully practicing authenticity."*

When I choose to be true to me, I have the power to shift my life and my culture around me.

Authenticity promotes connection and authenticity with vulnerabilty from others. When you choose to show up, to know and embrace what makes you different, you will feel better about yourself, you bring your truest self to your actions and invite others to the same. You live out of a place of boldness and God-confidence.

When you are real, you are inviting others into realness just by being you. There is so much beauty in someone that has put the mask of pretense down and shows up.

Dare! Dare to step outside your comfort zone. Do what scares you

In a movie I watched this one sentence struck me:

> *"Why are you trying so hard to fit in when you are born to stand out?"*

> *"Whatever you can do or dream you can, begin it, Boldness has a genius, power and magic in it. Begin it now"* - Johann Wolfgang Goethe

I am excited for you in the next weeks, months, and years. You will continue to grow where you keep your heart open. Never forget that you have a purpose on this earth.

Chapter 10 | Beautiful Authentic You

You are beautiful just the way you are.
You are loved and so beautifully worthy of love.

"Continue to let Jesus whisper His love over you, continue to spend time with Him each and every day. He is the Master Designer of your life. He is the boldness that flows from you with God-confidence. Go after Him and what He delights in as this will in turn be your delight. Know that He delights in relationship with you, in showing you each and every day His wondrous love for you."

One final song by Brandon Lake - Let God's love wash over you as you reflect on His goodness and extravagant love for you.

[Lost In Your Love (feat. Sarah Reeves) - Brandon Lake | House of Miracles](#)

SELF-CARE

Do something for you and for someone you love.

Buy a friend a coffee. Get a massage for yourself. Have a spa night at home with a friend. Read a book in a hot bubble bath with candles. Get away for a night. Spoil yourself and feel loved and worthy.

HOMEWORK

Do something that scares you.

Do something that makes you laugh in delight.

All those words that you have had said about you, those affirmations. Your truth, put them on a wall where you can see them and be constantly reminded every day of your truth.

A PRAYER FOR YOU TODAY

"Papa, this beautiful and amazing woman has been on a journey the last 10 weeks to learn, grow and discover more about who You have made her to be. I pray that she will continue to grow and learn, that she will hear Your voice whisper love, acceptance and grace over her. I pray that she will begin to see herself as You see her. Papa, and experience a joy that she has never experienced before. Saturate her with Your love. I pray she will experience delight as she continues to draw near to you and learn a deeper love. Guide her and give her wisdom in all her decisions. Surround her with a tribe of friends that pull out the gold in her that you have put there. And as she gives back into the world Papa, let her know she walks with you and is a light to those around her. Give her the courage and bravery to speak and act with Your boldness. Thank you for this beautiful woman and the impact she has on the world around her. Amen."

References

"CliftonStrengths Online Talent Assessment | EN." Gallup, 20 September 2019, www.gallup.com/cliftonstrengths. Accessed 22 March 2023.

About The Author

Ellen Reimer is a Registered Professional Counselor, Personal Life Coach, a mom to 4 men and is a woman with a burning desire to see others live life with purpose and zeal, confident in knowing who God made them to be..

Through Ellen's own journey she found that 'growth happens outside the comfort zone' she stepped outside of a life of 'religion within community' to a world unknown with her small family.

She came to understand the importance and freedom in healing pain from the past, embracing her story and becoming the woman God designed her to be.

Ellen's purpose and mission is to see women find this freedom, to live with passion, purpose and walk in the love and wisdom of everything that God placed inside each of them.

Throughout this workbook you will find many of the same tools that Ellen used in her own journey of healing and learning the extravagant love God has for her.

www.ingramcontent.com/pod-product-compliance
Lightning Source LLC
Chambersburg PA
CBHW080324080526

44585CB00021B/2458